BIRMINGHAM TROLLEYBUSES

David Harvey
Series Editor Robert J Harley

MP Middleton Press

Front cover: Leyland no. 71 stands on the cobbles of Yardley trolleybus station on 30th June 1951, which was the final day of operation. It is working on the 92 service to Albert Street and, bearing in mind that it would be towed away for scrapping later during the day, it looks in remarkably good condition. (L.W.Perkins)

Rear cover: A trio of trolleybuses wait in line astern within yards of the terminus of the 94 route during the last year of operation. Leading the queue is 1934 six wheeler no. 44 (OC 1144). The metal framed MCCW bodies were among the first to be fitted to trolleybuses in Britain and the order for 50 trolleybuses in a single batch was briefly the largest ever placed, until the 1934 orders placed by London Transport. The two four wheelers are a Leyland TB5 and a 2½ years' younger TB7. (Stratford Guild Library)

Cover colours - Cobalt blue and primrose/cream represent the livery of the Birmingham trolleybuses.

Published November 2007

ISBN 978 1 906008 19 2

© Middleton Press, 2007

Design Deborah Esher

Published by
    Middleton Press
    Easebourne Lane
    Midhurst
    West Sussex
    GU29 9AZ
Tel: 01730 813169
Fax: 01730 812601
Email: info@middletonpress.co.uk
www.middletonpress.co.uk

Printed & bound by Biddles Ltd, Kings Lynn

CONTENTS

1. Nechells Route
- 1   Old Square
- 12   Aston Street
- 14   Bloomsbury Street
- 18   Nechells Park Road
- 24   Washwood Heath Depot

2. Coventry Road Route
- 26   Albert Street to Digbeth
- 40   Station Street
- 47   Deritend
- 60   Coventry Road Depot
- 65   Small Heath
- 71   Hay Mills
- 76   The Swan
- 85   South Yardley
- 89   Sheldon
- 103   Lode Lane

- 108   Rolling Stock
- 116   The End and After

INTRODUCTION AND ACKNOWLEDGEMENTS

Thanks are due to all the photographers whose pictures are included in this volume. These gentlemen, who are credited in the text, were active in the years prior to June 1951 and provided a wealth of material, much of which has not been published before. Special thanks are due to Peter Townsend who drew the detailed overhead map of the Birmingham system. Finally, thank you to my wife Diana, who allowed me time to write the manuscript and who proof read the completed draft.

HISTORICAL BACKGROUND

The Birmingham trolleybus system was basically two unconnected routes. The Nechells route was 2.44 miles long and was the 14th system to open in Britain. The Coventry Road route initially to Yardley was 5.23 miles and had an extension to the city boundary, Sheldon of 2.51 miles. The Lode Lane branch of 1.5 miles was the only British trolleybus route to be opened under the wartime Emergency Powers Act. At its maximum the system was 10.18 miles/16.3km long. Over the 28 years of operation, a total of 114 trolleybuses was operated with a maximum fleet strength of 90 vehicles. Birmingham was the 16th largest out of 50 trolleybus systems in Britain. The Nechells route was the first trolleybus service to replace a tram route and the closure of the system on 30th June 1951 was the first post-war abandonment and took place before final tramway closure in the city.

The Nechells tram route was never economical and with the track in a poor state of repair, in 1921 it was decided to experiment with 'trackless trolleys'. The Transport Committee and the General Manager went to Bradford to look at two experimental top-covered double-deck trolleybuses, which were being operated. As a result of this visit, the decision was made to convert the Nechells trams to trackless trolleybuses. The application to replace the trams with trolleybuses was granted after the order for the vehicles was placed. The Birmingham Corporation Act 1922, Part IV, subtitled 'Trolley Vehicles, Tramways and Omnibuses' overcame the reluctance and objections of the Board of Trade to allow top covered double deck buses. The order was placed with Railless of Rochester in August 1921 to supply twelve 42 hp double deck F12 chassis that were fabricated by Short Brothers. The body order went to Charles Roe of Crossgates, Leeds, for top covered, outside staircase, fifty-one seater bodies costing £36,000.

The new route was from Old Square to the Nechells terminus at the junction of Cuckoo Road and Long Acre. The Railless LFs were numbered 1-12 (OK 4823-4834) and improved the service enormously. There was a four minute headway on the service with an average of seven stops per mile and an average speed of ten miles an hour. The overhead wires were initially spaced 13"/330mm apart on the Nechells route, as opposed to the later 18"/657mm.

In 1926, three more trackless Railless LFs, built with Short bodies were delivered as 14-16 (ON 2825-2827). The final solid tyred trackless was an AEC 607 chassis. It had a Vickers H26/26RO body and entered service on 3rd March 1926. It was numbered 17 (ON 3261) and had a foot operated accelerator and brake.

By 1930 it was becoming obvious that the solid tyred Railless fleet was due for replacement. Most of the 1-12 class had already run just over 200,000 miles and had received two overhauls, while the other four trackless trolleys (14-17), although only four years old, were unfashionable with their outside staircases and solid tyres.

An order was placed in the summer of 1931 with Leylands for the first production batch of ten four wheeled TBD1 trolleybuses, although this was amended in October to eleven. The need to support local industry during the Depression years favoured the Leyland/GEC combination and for this reason the body order was also placed locally with John Buckingham, the Birmingham bodybuilder. Unfortunately, this Bradford Street based company went out of business due to the depression and the order was then transferred to Short Brothers who were building bus bodies for BCT.

The Leyland trolleybuses again looked like the standard Birmingham motor bus of the day. The new trolleybuses were numbered 1-3/5-7/9-11/13/15, with matching registration numbers, starting with OV 4001 etc. The missing fleet numbers, 4 and 8, were still in use as two Railless trolleybuses. The eleven half cab bodied trolleybuses entered service in February 1932.

It was announced in February 1932 that an order for five new six wheeled 663T trolleybuses had been placed. They each had an English Electric 80 hp motor and Brush H33/25R bodies on the Nechells route. The quintet entered service as nos 12-16 in August and September 1932 and the Birmingham trolleybus system settled down for a short period of stability. By 1932 the tram track along the main arterial Coventry Road was desperately in need of renewal and it was decided that trolleybuses should replace the trams. In May 1933 an order for fifty six wheeled Leyland TTBD2 trolleybuses was placed, powered by WT254 65 hp motors. The all-metal bodies were fifty-eight seaters built by MCCW. The batch of trolleybuses was numbered 17-66.

At the end of October 1933 one of the new trolleybuses was seen in the Old Square painted in grey primer. It was initially used for clearance tests. From mid-November, the new trolleybuses were delivered from Metro-Cammell. The Coventry Road overhead was completed by December 1933.

The new service began without ceremony on 5 January 1934. The conversion from trams to trolleybuses was seen as a great success! Increased headway to just two minutes, higher revenue and a new state-of-the-art fleet of trolleybuses offered the public a fast, reliable and comfortable mode of transport along Coventry Road for the first time in many years.

Sheldon was taken over by Birmingham in 1931 and within five years the Corporation constructed over one thousand council houses in the suburb. This made the extension of the trolleybus route from Yardley into Sheldon fairly urgent. The terminus of the new extension was to be at the Tiger's Island boundary, but because of the lack of a suitable turning point, the terminus was located at Arden Oak Road, just short of Hatchford Brook, some 0.4 miles inside the city boundary.

The extension was opened on Monday, 5th July 1936. Route numbers 94 to Albert Street and 95 to Station Street were used, although the latter was a peak hour service which did not operate at all on Sundays. The section from Yardley to Sheldon added 2.51 miles to the existing route along Coventry Road. The Sheldon extension required further trolleybuses to maintain frequencies over the longer distance. In September 1936, twelve four wheeled Leyland TB5 chassis were ordered, with GEC WT2516J 80 hp motors. The body order went to Metro-Cammell and the twelve were delivered in September 1937 as nos 67-78.

The building of the New Coventry Road at Lyndon End in 1938 was the only major alteration to the system until after the outbreak of the Second World War.

The last Birmingham order for trolleybuses was placed in April 1939 with Leyland Motors for twelve TB7s. They were numbered 79-90 and they entered service in January and February 1940. The Birmingham trolleybus system appeared to be thriving. The Leyland TB7s were nominally replacements for the half cab Leyland TBD1s, which although only eight years old, had all amassed between 140,000 and 201,000 miles. At the end of the service on Leap Year Day 1940, Leyland half cabs 4-11 were withdrawn.

From about the time that the West Bromwich tram conversion negotiations had started in 1937, proposals had been made to abandon the tram system in the city within the next seven years but no mention was made of the two trolleybus routes and it was anticipated that the somewhat isolated trolleybus routes would continue intact, well beyond the final tramway closure. So the first closure came as something as a surprise. The remaining fourteen trolleybuses working on the Nechells service had still to gain access to the nearest point on the 7 route by travelling one and a half miles using the power trolley boom and a trailing skate in the tram rail. Any prospect of putting up negative overhead wires had been lost when the two Washwood Heath routes were converted to Fischer bow collectors in 1928 as the tramcar bow collector might have fouled the poles of any passing trolleybus.

The problems in gaining access to the trolleybus route at Bloomsbury Street must have been difficult enough in normal circumstances, but in wartime, at night and in the blackout it must have been something of a nightmare! The real problem was that Birmingham's trolleybuses used trolleywheels, which required that the overhead had to be regularly greased with graphite to ensure a good electrical contact. When the skate was used as the electrical return, the resulting contact was sometimes poor. This in turn led to a lot of pyrotechnics, which infringed the blackout regulations. The arcing of the Nechells trolleybuses on depot workings in the hours of darkness was an obvious problem, especially as the route ran towards the adjacent part of the Tame Valley that was being targeted by the German Luftwaffe! In view of the prospect of more air-raids, the decision was quickly made in mid-September 1940 to suspend the Nechells trolleybus service until hostilities ended. There was no intention to abandon the route! On 30th September 1940, the trolleybuses ran a normal service throughout the day, returned to Washwood Heath depot at the end of the day and were replaced by diesel buses next day.

The 7 trolleybus route was replaced by motorbuses, with a route number of 43, to avoid confusion with the 7 bus route to Portland Road.

If the circumstances which caused the closure of the Nechells route were unique, the next change was also unusual. In the summer of 1941 the Ministry of Supply and War Transport provided the authority to build an extension from the Wheatsheaf, outside the Birmingham boundary, along Hobs Moat Road and Lode Lane to the new Rover factory. A trolleybus service was deemed to be a better option than running extra buses in Solihull UDC because of the need to conserve fuel oil and petrol.

The new 1.51 mile extension from Coventry Road was opened on 29th October 1941 into the grounds of the factory by way of a private road. Although initially the route was only worked to coincide with the Rover's work shifts, the trolleybuses were allowed to carry passengers other than Rover workers when space permitted. By December 1942 a regular hourly all day service was being operated. The new routes were numbered 96 from Albert Street and 97 from Station Street. After the war, the Lode Lane service was only run on Mondays to Fridays, except when the demands of the Rover factory required weekend workings.

After the end of hostilities, the fleet was repainted, but without the pre-war gold lining out. The evening of 15th April 1946 saw the introduction of hourly all night services on the main roads out of the city. Buses from Acocks Green garage were employed on Coventry Road's NS94A night service to Lyndon End. In reality, this was the yet to be introduced 99 trolleybus route extended from Station Street into the city by way of Hill Street to the terminus in Bull Street. The closure of the 84 and 90 Stechford tram routes on 2nd October 1948 caused congestion inside Coventry Road depot. The space occupied by the replacement Daimler buses was considerably more than that occupied by the trams.

The Lyndon End turn back became the last new section of trolleybus wiring to be opened on 24th January 1949. The ever increasing traffic demands on the trolleybuses had begun to cause rush hour difficulties at Arden Oak Road. The new Lyndon End overhead was used in the rush hour and was given the route number 99.

Although 24 of the trolleybuses were only between nine and twelve years old, the future of the trolleybus service along Coventry Road was in peril. The other key factors were that the overhaul facilities at Kyotts Lake Road would be closed down by 1954, after the withdrawal of the tramcars and towing trolleybuses to Tyburn Road bus works was not going to be really practical. Additionally the nationalisation of the Electricity Department meant that the cost of the electricity rose dramatically.

The trolleybus system closed down over the last two days in June 1951. On 29th June, the Rover Works service to Albert Street closed, while earlier in the day, the last Station Street service was worked. The following Saturday, 30th June, the final service left Albert Street at just before 11pm.

ROUTES

7. Old Square - Nechells
   Replaced tram route 7 on 27th October 1922 and closed on 30th September 1940.

56. Albert Street - Hay Mills
    Replaced tram route 56 on 7th January 1934 and closed on 30th June 1951.

57. Station Street - Hay Mills
    Replaced tram route 57 on 7th January 1937 and closed on 30th June 1951.

92. Albert Street - Yardley
    Replaced tram route 15 on 7th January 1937 and closed on 30th June 1951.

93. Station Street - Yardley
    Replaced tram route 16 on 7th January 1937 and closed on 30th June 1951.

94. Albert Street - Coventry Road (City Boundary, Sheldon)
    5th July 1936 to 30th June 1951.

95. Station Street - Coventry Road (City Boundary, Sheldon)
    5th July 1936 to 30th June 1951.

96. Albert Street - Lode Lane (Rover Works)
    29th October 1941 to 30th June 1951.

97. Station Street - Lode Lane (Rover Works)
    29th October 1941 to 29th June 1951.

98. Coventry Road (City Boundary, Sheldon)
    Cattell Road, 29th October 1951.

99. Albert Street - Coventry Road (Wagon Lane)
    24th January 1949 to 30th June 1951.

DEPOTS

WASHWOOD HEATH

This building was opened on 2nd May 1907 as a tram depot and was used for the Nechells trolleybuses from 27th November 1927, on routes 7, 8 and 9. Trolleybus service was suspended on 30th September 1940 and was not reinstated. The depot was partly used as a bus garage until closure as a tram depot on 1st October 1950 after the Washwood Heath and Alum Rock route abandonments. It remained a bus garage until closure by Travel West Midlands.

COVENTRY ROAD (ARTHUR STREET)

Arthur Street Depot opened on 24th October 1906 for trams and later became a part operational trolleybus depot on 7th January 1934, sharing accommodation with tramcars used on the Stechford routes. These closed down on 2nd April 1948, when buses replaced the trams. The depot was closed for trolleybuses on 30th June 1951, and survived as a WMPTE bus garage until October 1985.

KYOTTS LAKE ROAD WORKS

This location was opened as a CBT steam tram depot in May 1885; it was then acquired by BCT on 1st January 1907. It was converted to a tram overhaul works early in 1908. It was used for trolleybus overhauls from 1922 to 1929 and from 1934 to 1951. The building closed after the final tram abandonment and breaking up of tramcars by 1954.

TYBURN ROAD WORKS

Opened as a bus works in December 1929, this building was used for trolleybus overhauls from early 1930 until 1933. It was closed in 1995.

SAMPSON ROAD PAINTSHOP

Opened in 1925 and used as a paintshop until closure of Stratford Road routes in January 1937, this building served as tram storage until 1940. All Nechells trolleybuses were stored here from 1st October 1940 until June 1945. The building was vacated in September 1945.

Nechells Route Map

Probable layout of Saltley Road area

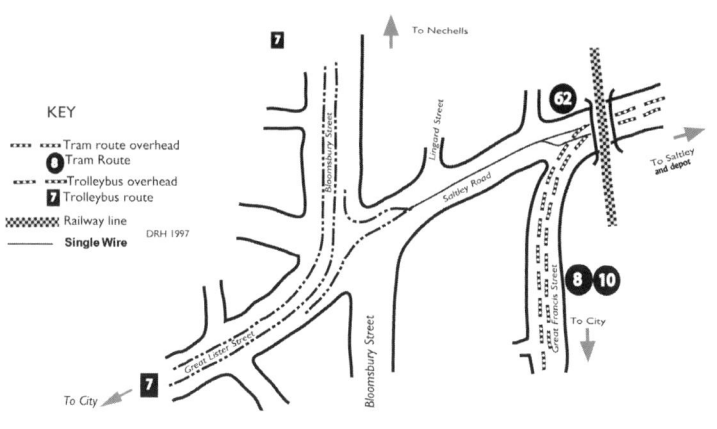

Enlargement of City Centre

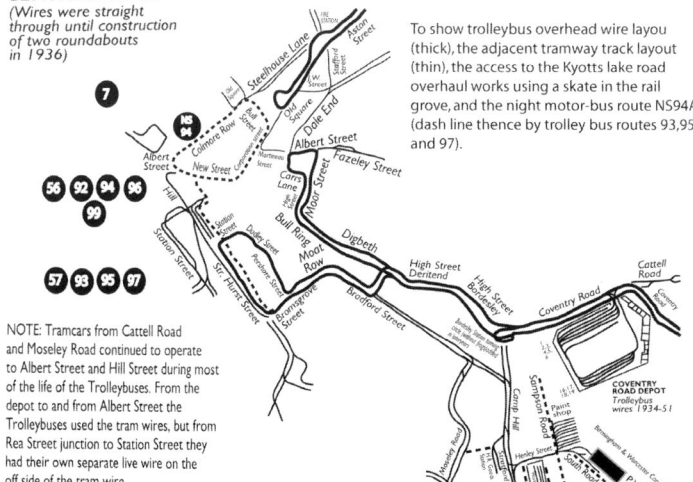

City centre

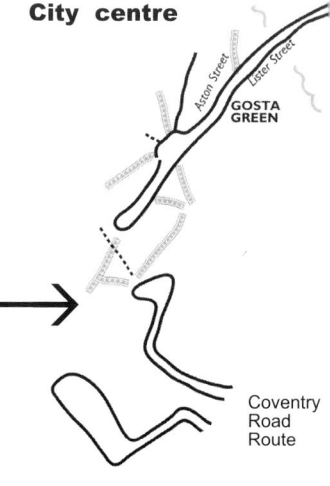

Coventry Road Route

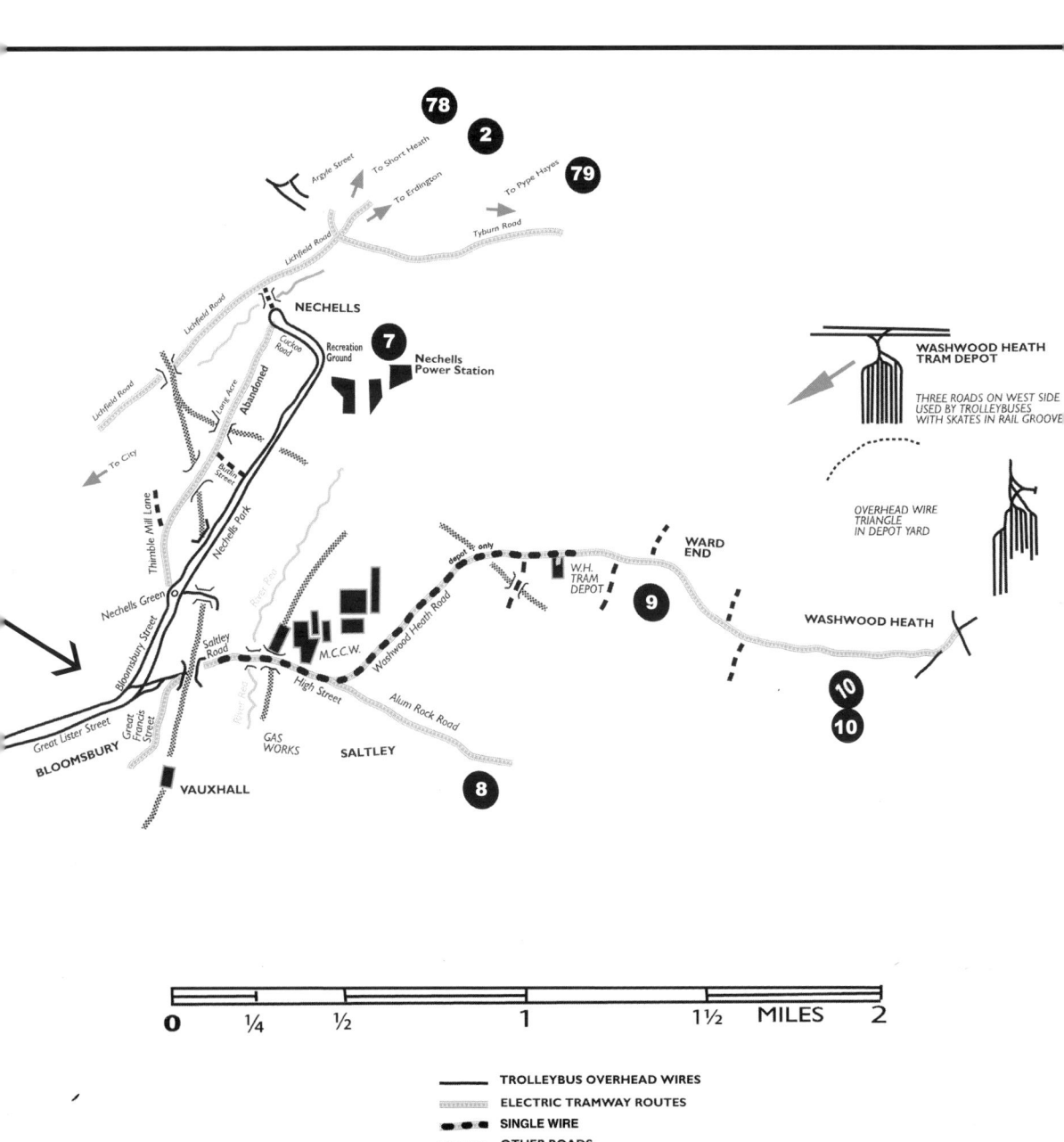

1. Nechells Route
OLD SQUARE

1.　Having turned from Corporation Street into Old Square, Railless F12, 5, (OK 4827), stands outside Lewis's new department store of 1929. The trolleybus is in the later livery with the rocker panels painted dark blue. The conversion of the tram route 7 to trolleybuses on 27th November 1922 led to a dramatic increase in passengers and revenue. In the last year of the trams they carried on average about 60,000 people, but by the summer of 1923 the numbers of passengers had gone up to about 91,000 which represented a 42.7% increase and receipts were up by 17.4%.
(E.N.Osborne)

2. The twelve Railless trolleybuses which opened the Nechells route were the first group of trolleybuses fitted with top covers in Britain. There had been other individual trolleybuses with enclosed top decks in Leeds and Bradford, but these were the first batch. Trolleybus 12 (OK 4832) turns around the central island in Old Square and is approaching the picking up stop outside Cranes musical instrument shop. (D.R.Harvey coll.)

3. When almost new in December 1922, Railless 10 (OK 4832) stands in Old Square in pristine condition, with the destination box showing NECHELLS 7. The Roe H25/26RO bodies on these Railless F12 chassis were 16'3½"/4965mm high and with their hand controllers and rubber tyres must have been really hard work for the drivers. This vehicle remained in service until 3rd February 1932. The original livery had the Corporation crest on the primrose painted rocker panels, as the blue area below the lower saloon windows was too narrow. (D.R.Harvey coll.)

4. Between 1929 and 1933, the trolleybuses were overhauled and repainted at the newly opened bus works at Tyburn Road. One of the first fruits of this movement away from Kyotts Lake Road Works was that the trolleybuses received the bus style livery with all the lower panels painted in dark blue, while the sloping canopy above the cab went the other way and was painted primrose. Trolleybus 7 (OK 4829) stands at the Old Square terminus in August 1929 in the new livery, which had been completed on 12th February 1929. (G.H.F.Atkins/J.Banks)

→ 5. An AEC 602 chassis bodied as a B36F vehicle by Strachan & Brown, though BCT records state Brush was the bodybuilder, was demonstrated on a sale or return basis from 17th August until late October 1923. No. 13 (OL 993) was a red and white coloured single decker. It amassed a total of 4,342 miles on the Nechells route. It stands at the City terminus in Old Square, before being returned to AEC. It later became Mexborough & Swinton's no. 31. (R.Marshall)

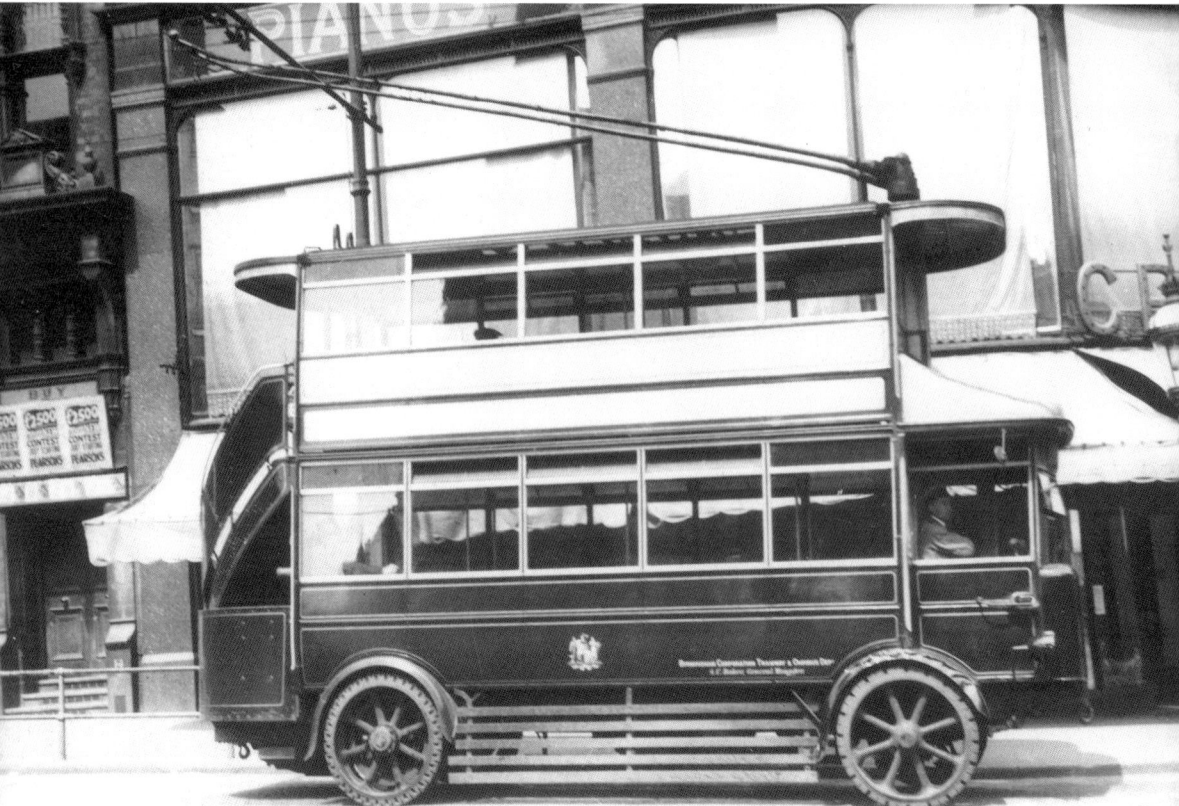

→ 6. All the eleven half cab Leyland TBD1 trolleybuses entered service in the first week of February 1932, but not before their Short bodies were lightened, as the first vehicle had failed the mandatory tilt test. This weight reduction entailed the elimination of a seat from the upper saloon, thus making the seating capacity H27/21R. The destination gear was removed and replaced by a paper destination sticker. No. 15 (OV 4015) was renumbered 8 later in February 1932, showing that it was only a few weeks old when photographed in Old Square. (R.Wilson)

DECORWALL Ltd

RADI
CALL AND SELECT YOUR
IBACH
PIANOS
NECHELLS
DV 4015
LIMITED

7. Fitted out with headlight masks, white painted body edges and a camouflaged roof, no. 78 (COX 78), a Leyland TB5 with a Metro-Cammell H29/24R body, stands in Old Square in early 1940. To the left of the bus is the Lewis's department store which replaced Newbury's Victorian building in 1933. The last half dozen of the 67-78 class were transferred to Washwood Heath Depot in September 1939 to augment the "indigenous" Nechells trolleybuses, but their stay would be for barely 12 months. (R.Wilson)

8. The original bodywork order for the Leyland TBD1 trolleybuses was placed with John Buckingham, a well known and well established Birmingham coachbuilder based in Bradford Street. They also had obtained an order for five AEC Regent 0661s, but Buckingham's fell victim to the depression and the trolleybus order went to Short Brothers. These trolleybuses were powered by 65hp GEC motors. Despite their somewhat old fashioned appearance, they had a good turn of speed. No. 11 (OV 4011) is leaving Old Square with the Newbury's store behind it. (D.R.Harvey Collection)

9. A demonstration trolleybus, a Guy-bodied Guy BTX, arrived in Birmingham on the 22nd February 1930 and stayed for 17 months. Numbered 18, it was registered in Wolverhampton as UK 8341, whereas its twin Guy BTX was numbered 19, stayed for just one week and yet perversely was registered in Birmingham as OG 9886. Demonstrator 18 (UK 8341) turns out of Old Square into Corporation Street in February 1930, when on its way to Nechells. (Guy Motors)

10.   Railless F12 trolleybus no. 11, (OK 4833), is about to turn right into Old Square from Corporation Street on 14th May 1931 and is waiting for the 1930s registered Austin Seven to clear the junction. Following the trolleybus along Corporation Street is a 1930 Vulcan bodied AEC Regent 661 motor bus. Piercing the sky line is the impressive tower of the Methodist Central Hall, which was opened in 1903. (D.R.Harvey coll.)

11. The prototype Leyland TTBD1 six wheeled demonstrator TJ 939 was given the fleet number 17, when it first came to Birmingham on 11th March 1933. Powered with a locally produced GEC WT 257 65 hp motor, it remained working almost entirely as a driver trainer on the Nechells route until the last day of July 1933, when it went back to Leyland Motors. No. 17 is being re-poled at the bottom of Corporation Street with the Victoria Law Courts just visible on the left. G.H.Rodway's car accessory shop and A.W.Iles's furniture store are just behind the trolleybus. TJ 939 came back to Birmingham for a second time between July and September 1936, when it was numbered 68. (D.R.Harvey coll.)

ASTON STREET

12. Passing the Swan with Two Necks public house and entering Aston Street from Central Place is trolleybus 17 (ON 3261). This solitary AEC 607 was fitted with a Vickers H26/26RO body and was the first trolleybus in the fleet to have a foot controller and the last to run on rubber tyres. The buildings on the left were soon to be replaced by the Central Fire Station. (W.H.Bett)

13. The new Central Fire Station and its associated shops have just been passed by four-wheeled Short bodied Leyland TBD1 trolleybus 6 (OV 4006). The trolleybus is on its way to Gosta Green, while beyond it is the grim urban landscape of Saltley and Nechells with back-to-back houses interspersed with factories and gas works. The shops with their canvas sunshades to the right of the trolleybus are on the corner of Gem Street. In the foreground is tram 307, inbound for Martineau Street when working on the 3X route. (D.R.Harvey coll.)

BLOOMSBURY STREET

14. Turning into Bloomsbury Street from Saltley Road is Railless trolleybus 5 (OK 4827). In front of the trolleybus is the Turks Head public house while on the right Wallis's grocery shop spills its wares onto the pavement. Above the trolleybus are two sets of running wires leading into Bloomsbury Street, but the sets of disconnected wiring were used to manoeuvre the trolleybuses when they were coming or going to Washwood Heath depot using a skate. (C.Carter)

15. Taken from a Guy Motors promotional film, Guy BTX UK 8341, numbered 18 by Birmingham, turns out of Washwood Heath Depot in February 1930. It can be seen that only the positive is attached to the overhead tram wire and that one of the depot mechanics is holding the skate in place, as the device passes over the tram points. Unlike OG 9886, this demonstrator had a curved staircase, so in view of the recently introduced straight staircase on motorbuses, it was surprising that UK 8341 stayed 15 months, while the straight staircase trolleybus lasted just one week. (Guy Motors)

16. Looking from the Inner Circle bus route in Nechells Place across High Park Corner and into Charles Arthur Street, reveals the Nechells trolleybus wiring going from Bloomsbury Street on the left into Nechells Park Road on the right. On the corner of Thimble Mill Road is the pet food store owned by E.H.Millward. (D.R.Harvey coll.)

17. Even as the tram lines on the Nechells route were being lifted, so the last trial runs of the Railless top covered trolleybuses were taking place. No.11 (OK 4833) crosses as far over as its trolleypoles will allow towards the offside of the road, as it negotiates the workmen in Nechells Park Road near High Park Corner in November 1922. Although displaying the destination SPECIAL CAR, the trolleybus appears to be full, possibly with civic dignitaries. (J.H.Taylforth coll.)

NECHELLS PARK ROAD

18.   Ascending Nechells Park Road, just before the opening of the trolleybus service to the public on 27th November 1922, is Railless F12 trolleybus 11 (OK 4833). It is near the crest of the steep hill which led from the Cuckoo Road terminus. The trolleybus' two 42 hp Dick Kerr motors would have made fairly light work of the hill, which was lined with mid-Victorian terraces. Those opposite Stanley Road had the luxury of front gardens. (J.H.Taylforth coll.)

19. One of the half cab trolleybuses, no. 2 (OV 4002), a nine year old Leyland TBD2 with a Short H27/21R body, is waiting at the terminus of the 7 route in Cuckoo Road, Nechells on 24th February 1940. The trolleybus had been refitted with its original destination boxes and the large headlight, although the latter had been masked as part of the wartime blackout restrictions. Trolleybuses 4-11 were withdrawn at the end of the month, when they were nominally replaced by the 79-90 batch, but 1-3 had been overhauled out of sequence and were still operational, when the Nechells service was abandoned. (L.W.Perkins)

→ 20. The most elusive members of Birmingham's trolleybus fleet were the 1932 batch of five Brush bodied AEC 663Ts. These 58 seaters were numbered 12-16 and 13 (OJ 1013) was the first one to enter service on 19th August 1932. Along with all the others, it was withdrawn on 30th September 1940, having run a total of 227,376 miles. Somewhat surprisingly, in view of the wartime shortages of trolleybuses elsewhere, it was put into Sampson Road North paintshop, until broken up in June 1945. No. 13 is standing at the Cuckoo Road terminus on 27th February 1940. (L.W.Perkins)

→ 21. In September 1939, the last three of the COX registered Leyland TB5 trolleybuses were transferred to Washwood Heath Depot to augment the existing Nechells vehicles. No. 77 (COX 77) stands outside the Victorian terraces at the Nechells terminus of the 7 route on 24th February 1940, a few days before being returned rather suddenly to resume its duties on Coventry Road's services. (L.W.Perkins)

22. Another of the COX registered trolleybuses stands outside the Cuckoo Road houses, some of whose residents have come out to look at the vehicle. No. 78 (COX 78) had been recently repainted returning to service on 29th April 1940 and looks in pristine condition with white blackout markings that, for once, actually enhance the appearance of the vehicle. The trolleybus, however, has yet to have its roof painted in camouflage grey. (Commercial postcard/G.Kelland)

23. Trolleybus no. 1 (OV 4001), the first of the Leyland TBD1s, has just left the Cuckoo Road terminus and is turning into Nechells Park Road on Tuesday, 27th February 1940, as it passes the Ind Coope & Allsopp public house of the same name. The distant Nechells terminus was located among the Victorian houses that adjoined the heavily industrialised valley of the River Tame. This industrial area was to play a major part in the decision to close down the Nechells trolleybus service. (L.W.Perkins)

WASHWOOD HEATH DEPOT

24. The Electro-Magnetic Brake Company of West Bromwich only ever made one trolleybus and it was one of the most advanced vehicles ever built. Numbered 13 (OL 4636), the chassis was remarkably low, with only one step from road to lower saloon with two drive shafts outside the chassis frame. The Roe body was also advanced, having a totally enclosed platform and staircase. It had a short life operating for the Corporation from 10th April 1924 to 1st April 1926 and it ran 20,894 miles before being returned to EMB and being promptly broken up. (H.A.Whitcombe coll.)

25. Trolleybus 4 (OV 4013) had its registration out of sequence because for the first month of its life it was numbered 13. The original number 4, a 1922 Railless F12 was still, albeit briefly, in service. Looking for all the world like a contemporary motor bus, these Short bodied Leyland TBD1s were well appointed, despite their unusual frontal appearance. The trolleybus had yet to enter service, as it is still equipped with a full set of destination equipment, which was removed when trolleybus number 1 failed the tilt test. (J.H.Taylforth coll.)

2. Coventry Road route

ALBERT STREET TO DIGBETH

26. Waiting at the top of Carrs Lane outside Jay's furniture store is no. 36 (OC 1136). This was one of the fifty MCCW bodied Leyland TTBD2 vehicles built for the conversion of the two Coventry Road services to Yardley, which took place on 7th January 1934. In 1951 it is standing at the City terminus of the 94 service next to the hexagonal trolleybus stop which was used only to unload passengers. (F.Lloyd)

27. GEC 65 hp motored Leyland TTBD2 six wheeler no. 20 (OC 1120) has left the setting down stop in Carrs Lane and is about to turn into High Street on its way to the 94 route pick up terminus in Albert Street. The trolleybus is empty, as passengers were not allowed to be carried between Carrs Lane and the pick up stop in Albert Street. (C.Carter)

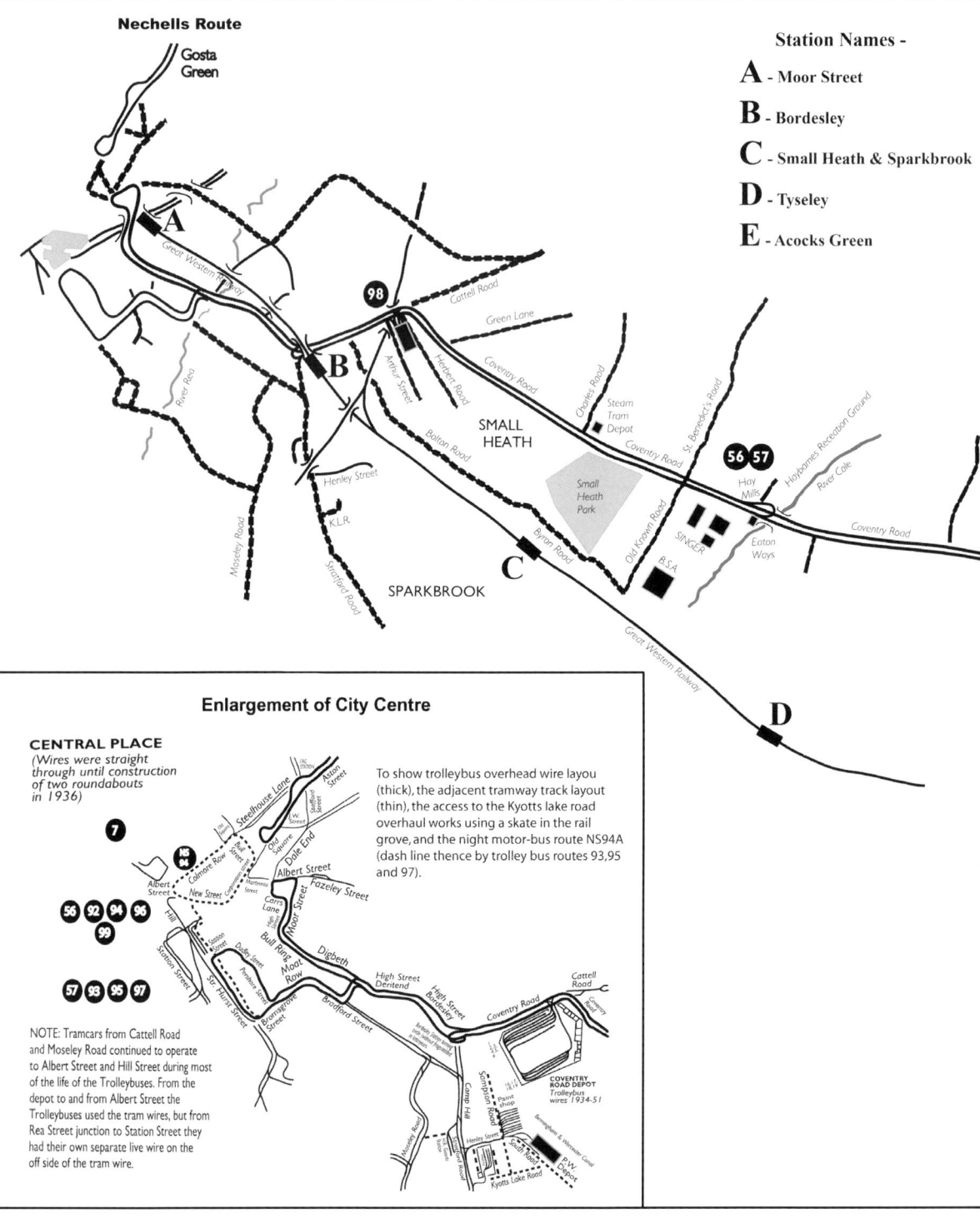

For details of the railway stations please
see the Middleton Press album
Stratford-upon-Avon to Birmingham.

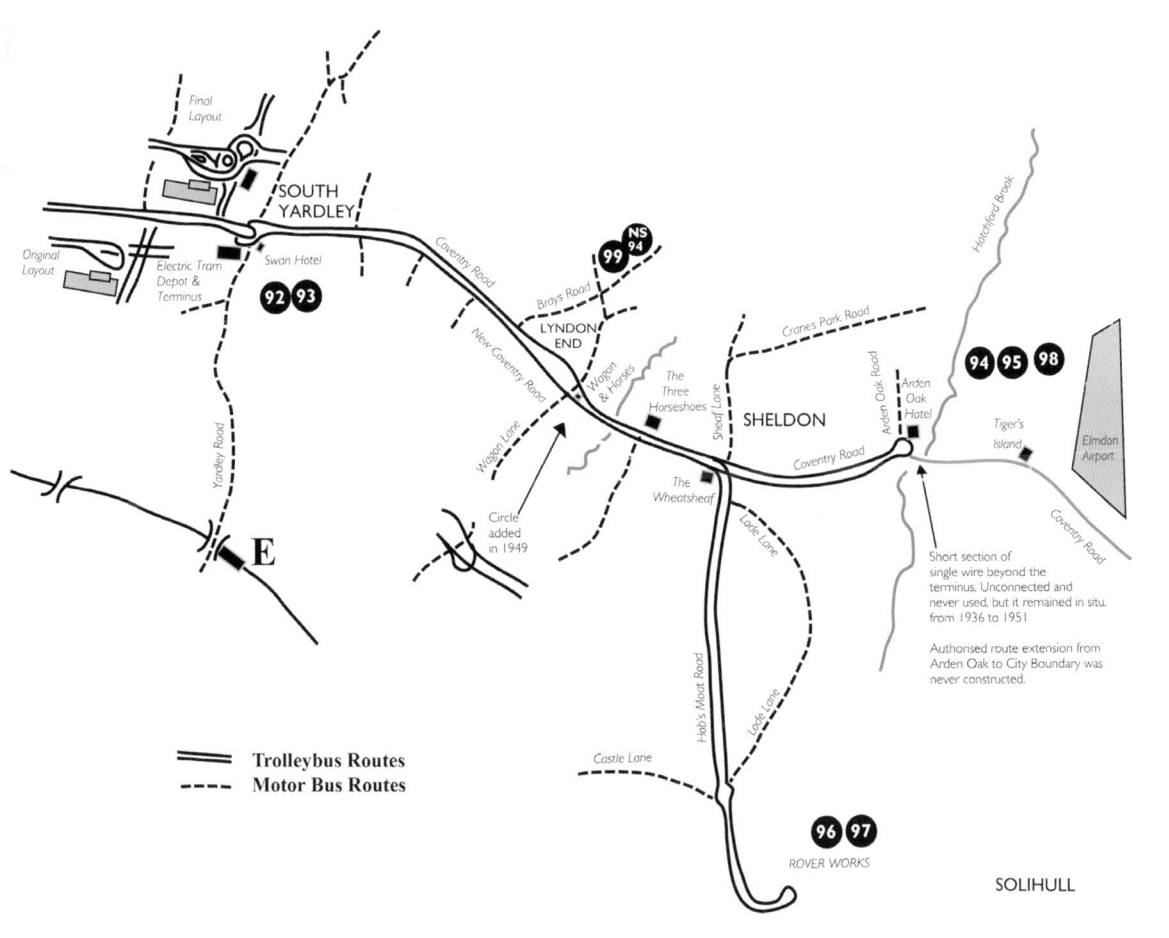

28. Still looking sound after eighteen years of service, Leyland trolleybus no. 32 (OC 1132) approaches the railings surrounding the subterranean toilets at the junction of High Street and Bull Street in the spring of 1951. The Belisha Beacons, without the later Zebra road markings, are in both High Street and Martineau Street. The trolleybus is passing the Phillips Furnishing Store, which had been Pattison's tea rooms and cake shop. On the left is the News Theatre advertising the latest newsreels from the Korean War. (D.R.Harvey coll.)

→ 29. During 1944, Metro-Cammell bodied Leyland six wheeler no. 22 (OC 1122) loads up with passengers outside the Beehive Warehouse department store before leaving on the 7 mile 1,300 yard/12.4km journey on the 94 service to Sheldon. The trolleybus has been painted with the wartime necessity of a camouflaged grey roof and rear dome and white edging paint. It was the 58 seater capacity of these trolleybuses which was to be very useful during the Second World War, when they were required to carry so many war workers to the factories in the vicinity of Coventry Road. (Birmingham Central Reference Library)

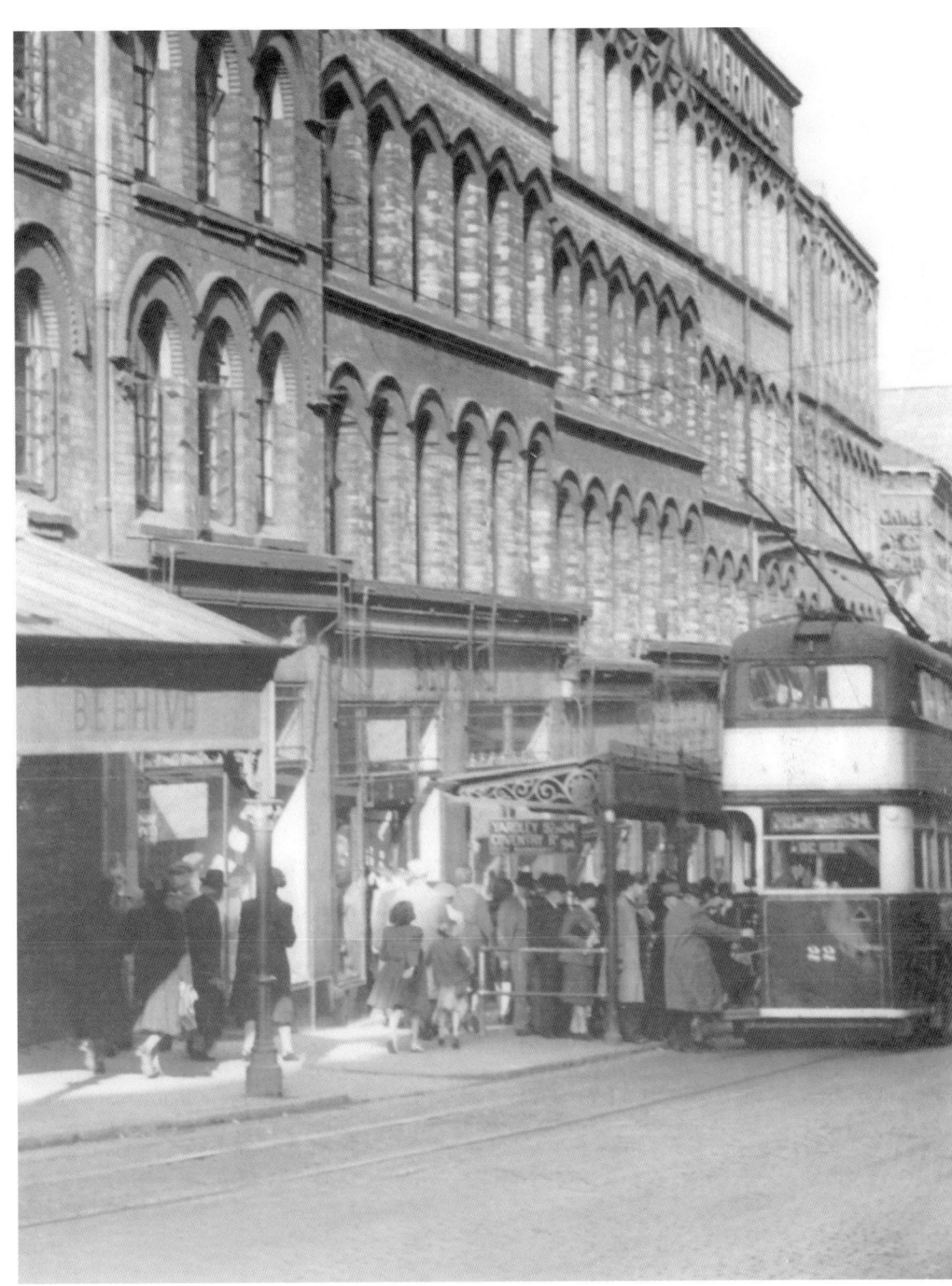

30. In the last month of the operation of the Coventry Road trolleybus service, the 94 route is being operated by no. 69 (COX 69), a Leyland TB5 powered with a 80 hp GEC motor and fitted with a 53 seat Metro-Cammell body. On the right the shop fronts of the Beehive are, as was usual on a sunny day, in deep shadow caused by the "corridor" of bus shelters which lined the eastern side of Albert Street. Opposite the trolleybus is an Austin K8 Three-Way 25 cwt van and, in front of it, is a Fordson E83W van. (D.R.Harvey coll.)

→ 31. The Beehive Warehouse was the last privately owned departmental store in the city centre and it survived for just over a century until closure on 29th February 1972. Trolleybus no. 24 (OC 1124) stands alongside the impressive shelters in Albert Street, when working on the 94 route to Small Heath, Yardley and Sheldon. By 1949, only the Moseley Road trams survived with the trolleybuses in Albert Street. Parked in front the Beehive is a 1934 Standard Twelve saloon.
(Birmingham Central Reference Library)

→ 32. Having turned hard right out of Albert Street, the 56, 92, 94, 96 and 99 trolleybus routes, using this city centre terminus, travelled up the hill in Moor Street, passing the lovely Georgian Dingley's Hotel, as they approached the junction with Carrs Lane. This is where the inbound trolleybuses turned to their unloading stop. Overtaking a Wolseley Series III 12/48 and a Morris Twelve Series III, is trolleybus no. 38 (OC 1138) on the 94 route in September 1950. It is looking remarkably smart after having received a light touch up and varnish on 9th June 1950. (R.Knibbs)

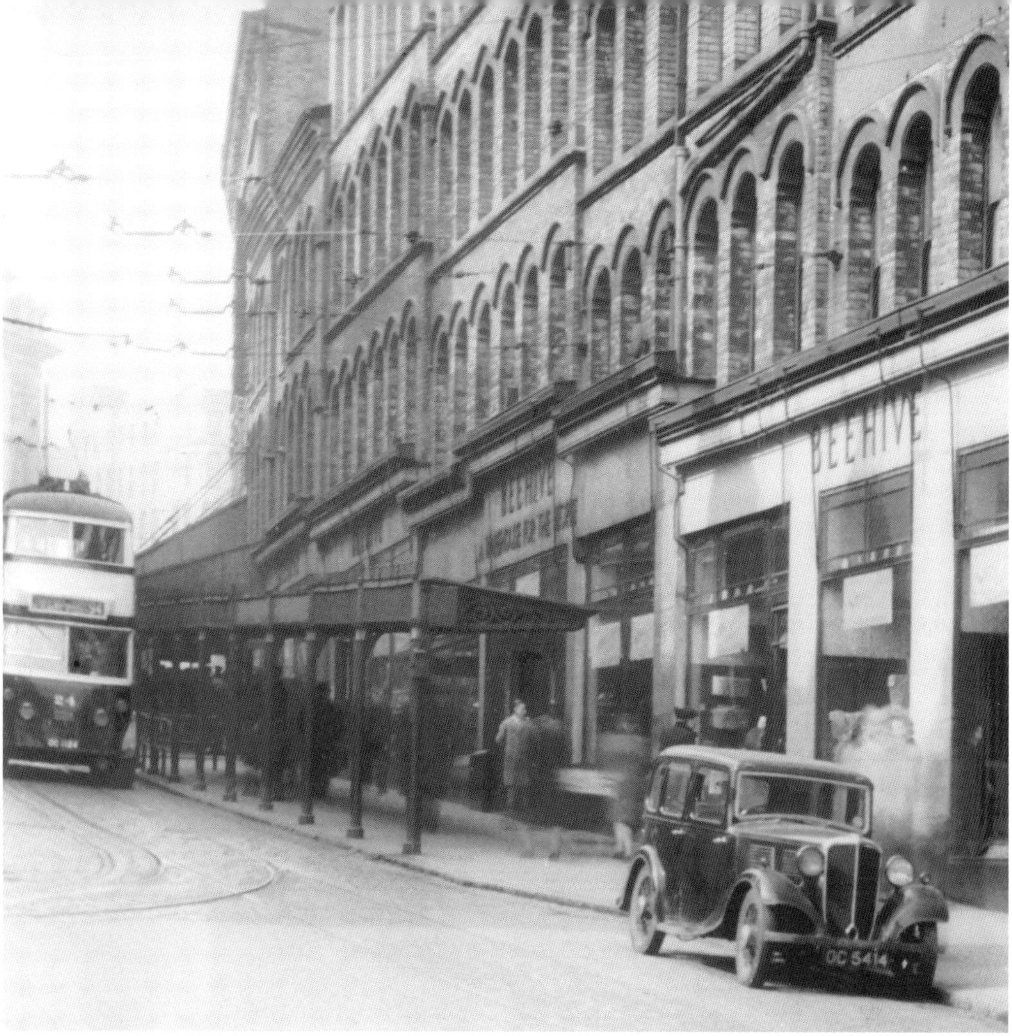
BEEHIVE
OC 5414

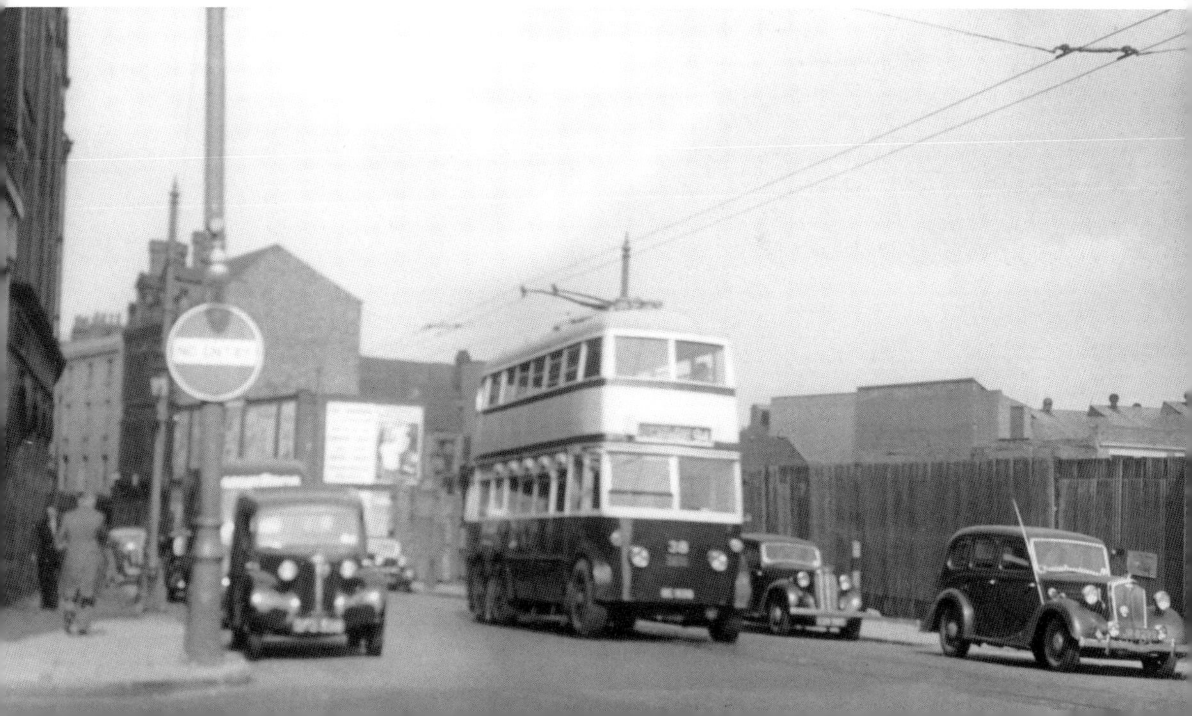

33. The impressive Moor Street Warehouse stood over the former Great Western Railway's tunnel, linking Moor Street Station with the main line terminus at Snow Hill. The shop was owned by the Norton family who, after trading for over 50 years, closed their premises in March 1964. The inbound trolleybus, no. 22 (OC 1122), garbed in the wartime livery, is dwarfed by these premises as it turns left into Carrs Lane by the half timbered Corner public house, before reaching its terminus just short of the junction with High Street. Parked on the left is a 1942 registered Fordson 2 ton van. (Birmingham Central Reference Library)

34. Standing in Moor Street opposite Oswald Bailey's Army and Navy Stores is trolleybus 27 (OC 1127), which is picking up passengers when working on the 94 route. When it moves away, it will turn sharp left into the Bull Ring. The trolleybus looks to have been recently repainted and, judging by the dark camouflaged roof of the distant bus and the number of soldiers, the repaint of 27 would have been its fourth overhaul, which put the vehicle back into service on 26th November 1946. (D.R.Harvey coll.)

35. Trolleybus 76 is turning from Moor Street into the Bull Ring, in front of the impressive Nelson House with Allen Griffiths' shoe shop on the ground floor and the True Vue television shop above. This Leyland TB5 had entered service on 24th September 1937. When new, these twelve four wheelers were as modern as anything else in service in Britain. They were equipped with metal framed MCCW bodies, traction batteries and a powerful 80 hp GEC traction motor. Almost new Daimler CVD6 2069 (JOJ 69) follows the trolleybus. (Stratford Guild Library)

36. A rather dusty six wheeled Leyland TTBD2 trolleybus, no. 41 (OC 1140), is being hauled by its driver, around the corner into Moor Street after the steep Bull Ring climb as it travels towards the Carrs Lane terminus of the 94 route. While the upper saloon, or OUTSIDE as it was termed on the side of the staircase, looks fairly empty, the lower saloon is loaded to the gunwales. Noticeable in the background near the junction with Park Street is how many of the buildings had been destroyed in the Second World War compared to the next photograph. (Stratford Guild Library)

→ 37. Leyland TTBD2 trolleybus 22 (OC 1122) is working on the original 92 service to Yardley in about 1935. The trolleybus, in its original gold lined out livery, has climbed up Bull Ring, having passed St Martin's Parish Church just to the right of where the people are queuing by the bus stop. Travelling down the Bull Ring is open balconied four wheel tramcar 420, which is working on the outbound 42 service to Kings Heath. The man with the gabardine coat, standing on the back platform of the trolleybus looks as if he is about to jump off the vehicle as it swings across into Moor Street. (A. Wilson)

→ 38. Having descended the Bull Ring on the ubiquitous 94 service, trolleybus no. 77 (COX 77) has passed the Lightfoot Refrigeration factory on the corner of Allison Street. The impressive marbled pillars guard the entrance to Digbeth Police Station which had been opened in 1911. The 67-78 class of Metro-Cammell bodied Leyland TB5 trolleybuses weighed 7 tons 6 cwt and sat 53 passengers. This was one seat less than the comparable Daimler COG5 bus, because their heavy traction batteries would have made them overweight. These batteries gave trolleybuses the ability to manoeuvre away from the overhead wires. (A.B.Cross)

MIDLANDS
42
EVENING
DESPATCH
420
22
GC 1122

CITY BOUNDARY
ALBERT STREET 94
GREY
77

39. Despite having received its fourth and final repaint during the previous February, on 24th July 1949, six wheeled Leyland 44(OC 1144) looks remarkably smart as it passes the Old Bull's Head in Digbeth. In the foreground are the soon to be made redundant tram tracks in Rea Street, used for the Moseley Road services as well as the Coventry Road trolleybus services, which terminated in Station Street. By the time of its withdrawal at the of end June 1951, trolleybus no. 44 had amassed 496,383 miles in nearly 17½ years service. (G.F.Douglas/A.D.Packer)

STATION STREET

40. A 1933 Coventry-registered Standard Ten overtakes the almost new Birmingham trolleybus no. 31 (OC 1131), which is moving slowly away from the distant Hill Street towards the terminus in Station Street. The trolleybus is working the 93 service to Yardley in February 1934 and is fitted with the original chain driven horizontal windscreen wipers. (D.R.Harvey coll.)

41. MCCW bodied Leyland TTBD2 trolleybus no. 20 (OC 1120) waits beneath the Bourn-vita advertisement in Station Street in 1949. This vehicle was one of the five of the class which were briefly placed in store after the wartime suspension of the Nechells route. It is working on the 93 route to the original Coventry Road trolleybus terminus in Yardley. (S.N.J.White)

42. The driver of no. 81 (FOK 81), one of the twelve 1940-built Leyland TB7s, has already turned his wheels so that, when he leaves this well hidden terminus, he can cut across Station Street in front of the Market Hotel and turn right into Dudley Street. Behind the trolleybus is the railway station, which had been built in 1883 on the site of a warren of some of the worst 18th century slums in Birmingham.
(R.Wilson)

→ 43. On the last day of service, 30th June 1951, a still smart looking trolleybus 49 (OC 1149) stands in Station Street, when being employed on the more usual 93 route shortworking from Station Street to Yardley. This 1934 Leyland TTBD2 with a 58 seat Metro-Cammell body is standing alongside the shelters, which bore a striking similarity to those found in the busier and more central trolleybus terminus in Albert Street. (G.B.Claydon)

→ 44. The trolleybus driver stands in the road, as if guarding his trolleybus from the enthusiasts standing on the pavement. Waiting in Station Street near to the vehicle entrance into New Street Station is trolleybus no. 90 (FOK 90). This Metro-Cammell bodied Leyland TB7, numerically the last Birmingham trolleybus, had been given a garage "spruce-up" at the end of May 1951 and was used on the two enthusiast tours on 3rd and 24th June, as well as closing the system. This is the second of those tours. (D.R.Harvey coll.)

YARDLEY AND
93
49
OC 1149

LONDON
EUSTON
BIRMINGHAM
LONDON
Osram
G.E.C.
SPECIAL
90

45.   MCCW bodied Leyland TB7, trolleybus 87 (FOK 87) has come out of Dudley Street and is about to go into Pershore Street on its way to Yardley on the 93 service. The trolleybuses only used this route on the outbound journeys. Towering above the trolleybus in this area devoted to the wholesale fruit and vegetable trade is the Sydenham Hotel, which had an Atkinson's owned public house on the ground floor. The car on the right is a 1948 Vauxhall 12/4 saloon. (R.Wilson)

46.   Standing at the head of a row of traffic in Bromsgrove Street is Metro-Cammell bodied Leyland TTBD2 32 (OC 1132). The trolleybus is waiting alongside the A.D.Wimbush bread and cake shop for the traffic lights to change, before following the tram tracks and turn right into Hurst Street on the way to the Station Street terminus of the 93 route. (R.Wilson)

DERITEND

47. Passing each other in Digbeth in 1950 are two Metro-Cammell 58 seat Leyland TTBD2 six wheel trolleybuses. Travelling into the City on the 94 service to Albert Street is no. 21 (OC 1121), whose driver is letting the bus bound for Moseley Road turn into Rea Street. Trolleybus no. 41(OC 1141), bound for Yardley and Sheldon, travels into Deritend. (R.H.G.Simpson)

48. On the last day of trolleybus operation, Leyland TTBD2 trolleybus no. 50 (OC 1150) is turning from Digbeth into Rea Street with Ridgway's household goods shop on the corner. These buses weighed 8 tons 17 cwt/8991kg despite being only 26ft/7924mm long, so turns like this were quite hard work for the driver! The trolleybus is working inbound on the 93 route to Station Street. (D.R.Harvey coll.)

← 49. Running empty back through Digbeth to the Coventry Road depot is trolleybus no. 20 (OC 1120) during May 1934, when the new Coventry Road trolleybus service was barely five months old. Some of the 33 leather covered seats can be seen in the upper saloon while on the roof of both trolleybuses are the electrical suppressors and the crawling boards to gain access to the trolley booms. Beyond the trolleybus and the tram is the junction with Rea Street. A Morris-Commercial "Dictator", no. 89 (OV 4089), has turned out of Rea Street on a 22 service to Bolton Road.
(Birmingham City Transport)

50. On the last day of operation of BCT trolleybuses, a Leyland six wheeler crosses the line of the River Rea, as it passes from Digbeth into High Street Deritend, with the Floodgate Street junction on the left. The trolleybus is working on the 92 route from Albert Street to Yardley. Travelling inbound on the 44A route from Acocks Green, and being partially masked by the Austin A40 van, is a barely one year old Guy "Arab" III Special which, like the trolleybus, has a Metro-Cammell body.
(G.B.Claydon)

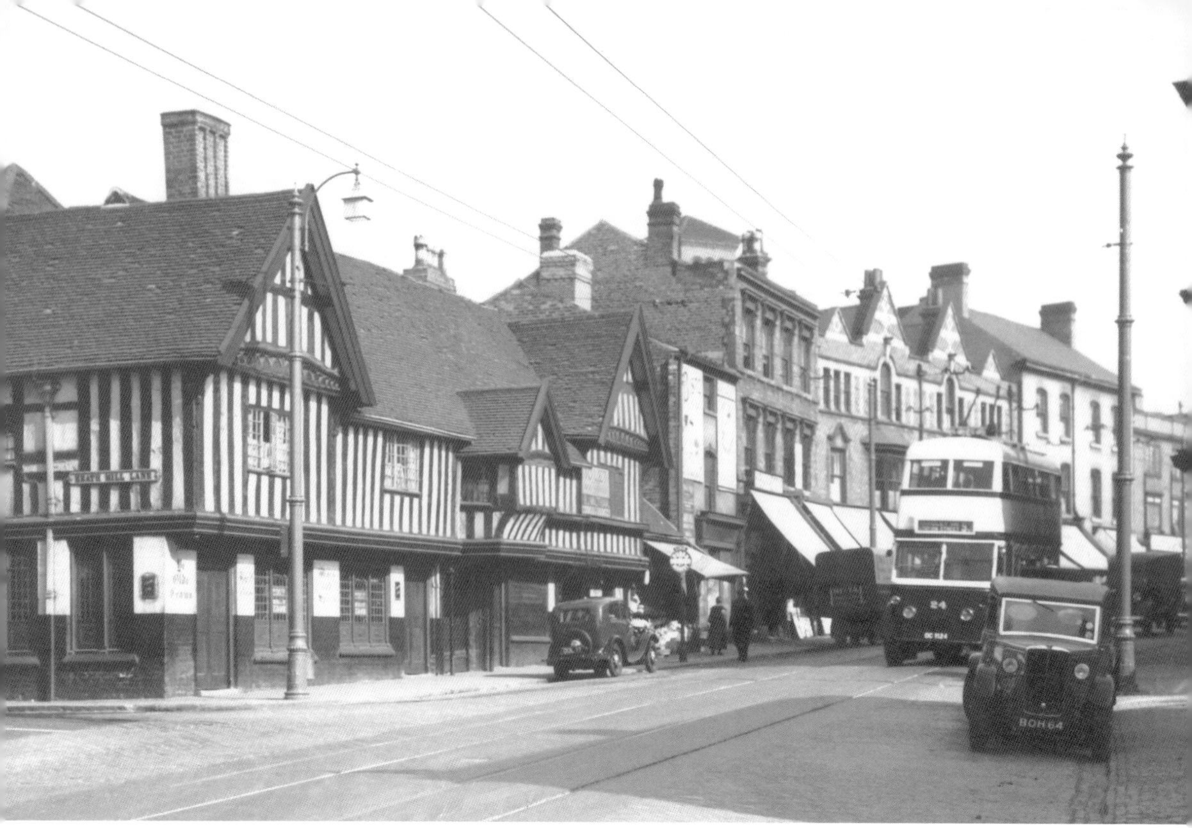
BOH 64

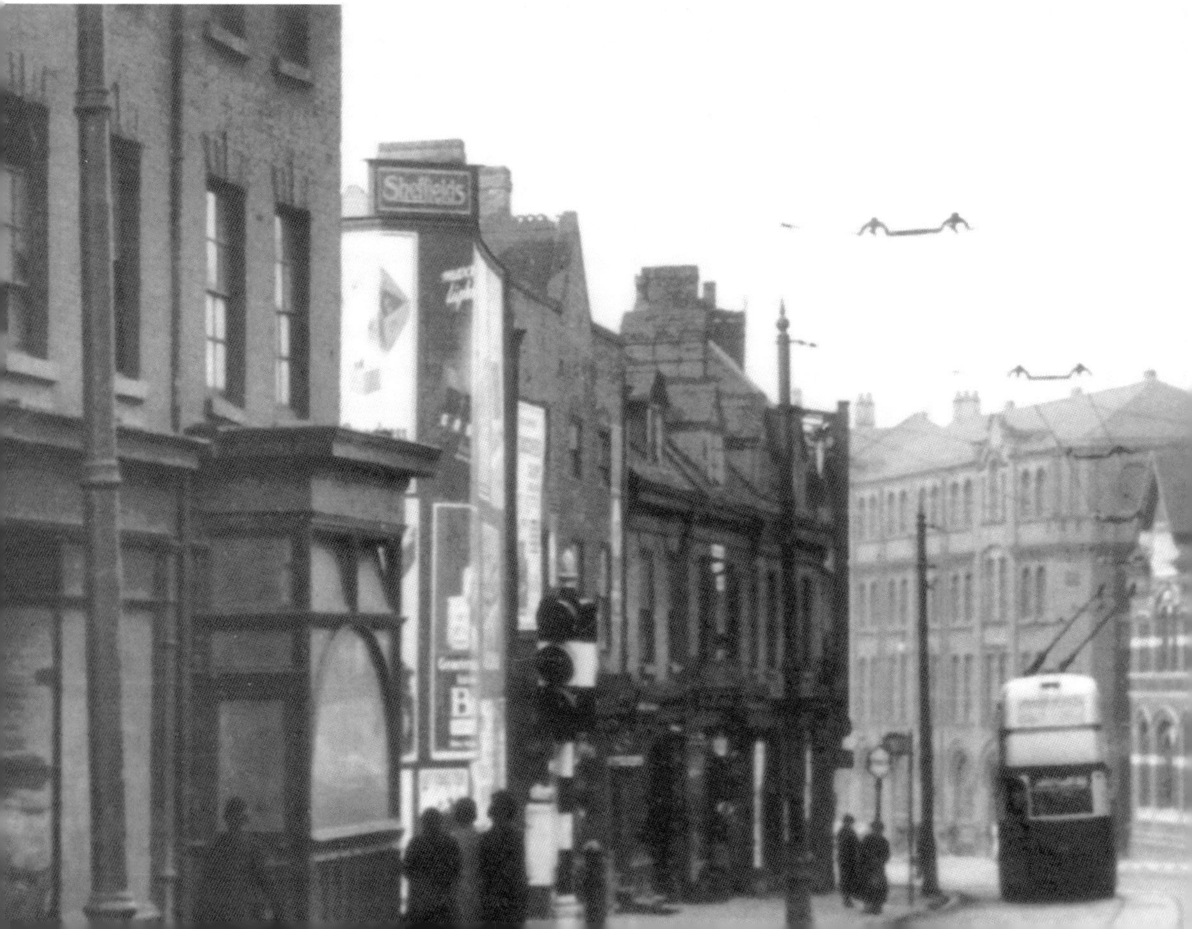
Sheffields

← 51. A brand new Morris Eight Series II car registered in September 1937 is parked outside the Old Crown in Deritend. This was built in 1368 as a mansion house and was enlarged with splendid Elizabethan half timbered additions. By 1700 it had become the first coaching inn in Birmingham and in the mid-19th century had become an enlarged Victorian pub. Travelling into the City on the 93 route is MCCW bodied Leyland TTBD2 trolleybus no. 24 (OC 1124).
(Birmingham Central Reference Library)

← 52. A Leyland TTBD2 has travelled down the hill in the rather rundown looking High Street, Bordesley in late 1938 when working on a City bound 93 service. It has gone through the traffic lights at the Alcester Street junction and has just left the trolleybus stop opposite the Old Crown public house. The large brick building beyond the trolleybus is the Bird's custard factory. (Birmingham Central Reference Library)

53. Passing the anti-blast walls in front of the Fisher and Ludlow factory in High Street, Bordesley during 1948 is the last of the 1934 six wheelers, 66 (OC 1166). It has just left the gloom of the Bordesley railway bridge and is travelling inbound on the 94 service. No. 66 is being followed by a tram working on the soon to be abandoned 84 route from Stechford. Behind the trolleybus is Camp Hill, which the trolleybuses traversed when going to Kyotts Lake Works. No. 66 was the only one of the batch to be fitted with traction batteries. (J.S.Webb)

54. Trolleybus no. 31 (OC 1131) is using the half connected loop opposite the Coventry Road junction in High Street, Bordesley. The trolleybus is being returned from being overhauled at Kyotts Lake Road Works in May 1946. Mechanics with wooden pole retrievers are standing at the rear of the trolleybus in order to manoeuvre it across High Street so as to gain the out of City wires. The loop was only connected at the one end and required a lot of skill from the driver to complete the exercise. The loop was occasionally used on match days at St Andrew's football ground to turn trolleybuses for outbound football specials. (D.R.Harvey coll.)

55.   Turning into Kyotts Lake Road Works on 5th April 1950, where trolleybus overhauls took place, is Leyland TTBD2 six wheeler 47 (OC 1147). It had gone to the works to have its shackle pins and body bearers repaired. The trolleybus had run over the tram tracks from Camp Hill at the junction with Coventry Road and along Stratford Road to Kyotts Lake Road. The trolleybus used the positive tram overhead wire and returned the current by way of a chain skate fitted on to the tracks which is visible behind the trolleybus. (G.F.Douglas/A.D.Packer)

56.   One of the most evocative places on the Birmingham system was where the trolleybuses emerged from the stygian gloom of Bordesley Bridge. The wide bridge over Coventry Road carried the former GWR mainline from Snow Hill to Paddington while on the right was Bordesley Station. On the last day of operation, Leyland six-wheeler no. 60 (OC 1160), working on the 58 route, leads the Elmdon Airport bus no. 2260 (JOJ 260), an MG Midget and in the distance Leyland TB7 trolleybus no. 79 (FOK 79) towards the City centre. Above the trolleybus is a second set of detached trolleybus wires, which had been used until 1937 to allow trolleybuses to turn left to reach the works at Kyotts Lake Road. (L.W.Perkins)

57. The dark, damp double width bridge underneath Bordesley Station, Coventry Road looked much the same some 45 years later. On 21st July 1996, the author took his bus (no. 2489 - JOJ 489) to the point where the Crossley bus has just emerged from beneath the railway bridge on its way out of the City on a 94 service. (D.R.Harvey)

→ 58. Ten trolleybuses, led by the first of the 1940 batch of Metro-Cammell bodied Leyland TB7s, no. 79 (FOK 79), stand on Kingston Hill, Coventry Road on 8th June 1949. To the right are the late 1930s maisonettes, while the large building in the background was J&W Mitchell's paper mill. The trolleybuses are each awaiting their turn to be driven about two hundred yards up the hill and turn right into Coventry Road depot. (G.F.Douglas/A.D.Packer)

→ 59. Passing the entrance to Coventry Road depot on 16th June 1951, when working a City bound 94 service, is no. 78 (COX 78), the last of the 67-78 batch of Leyland TB5s. They only sat 53 because they were the first class of trolleybuses fitted with heavy traction batteries to enable them to move independently away from the trolleybus overhead. Behind the trolleybus is the M & B owned Greenaway Arms public house, standing in the angle of Coventry Road to the right and Cattell Road, which was the route of the former tram line to Stechford. (L.W.Perkins)

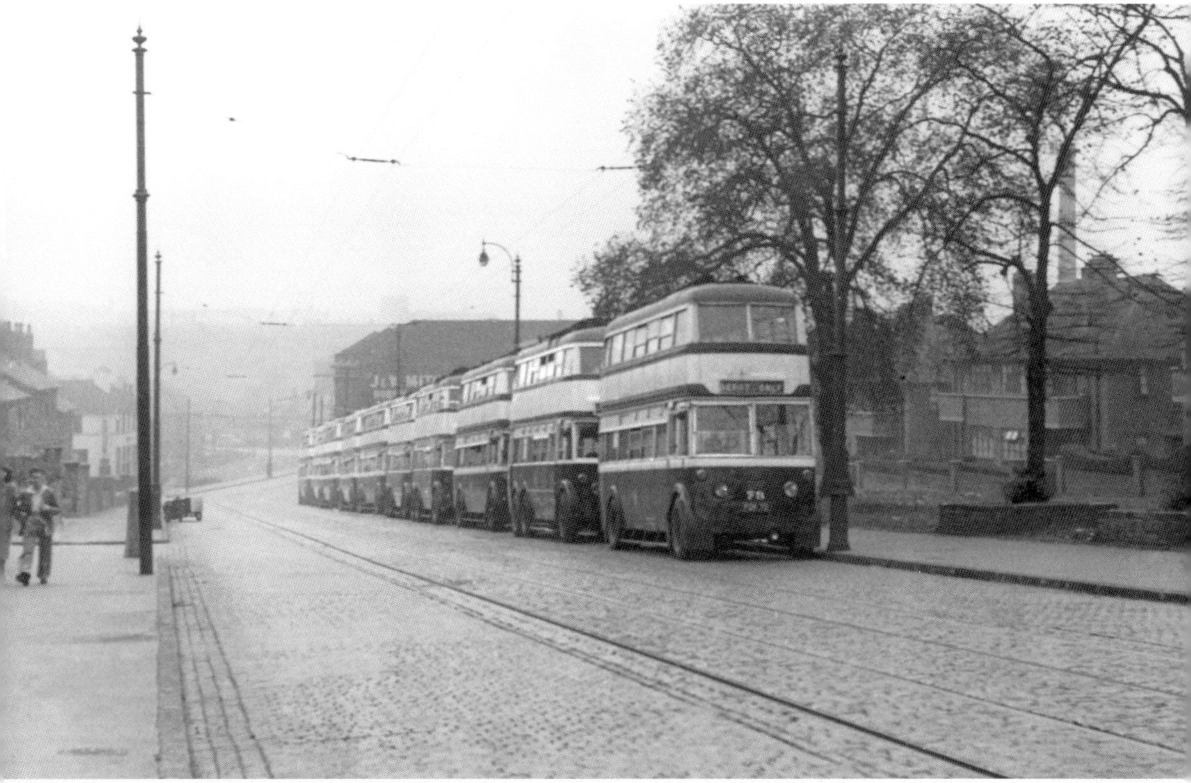

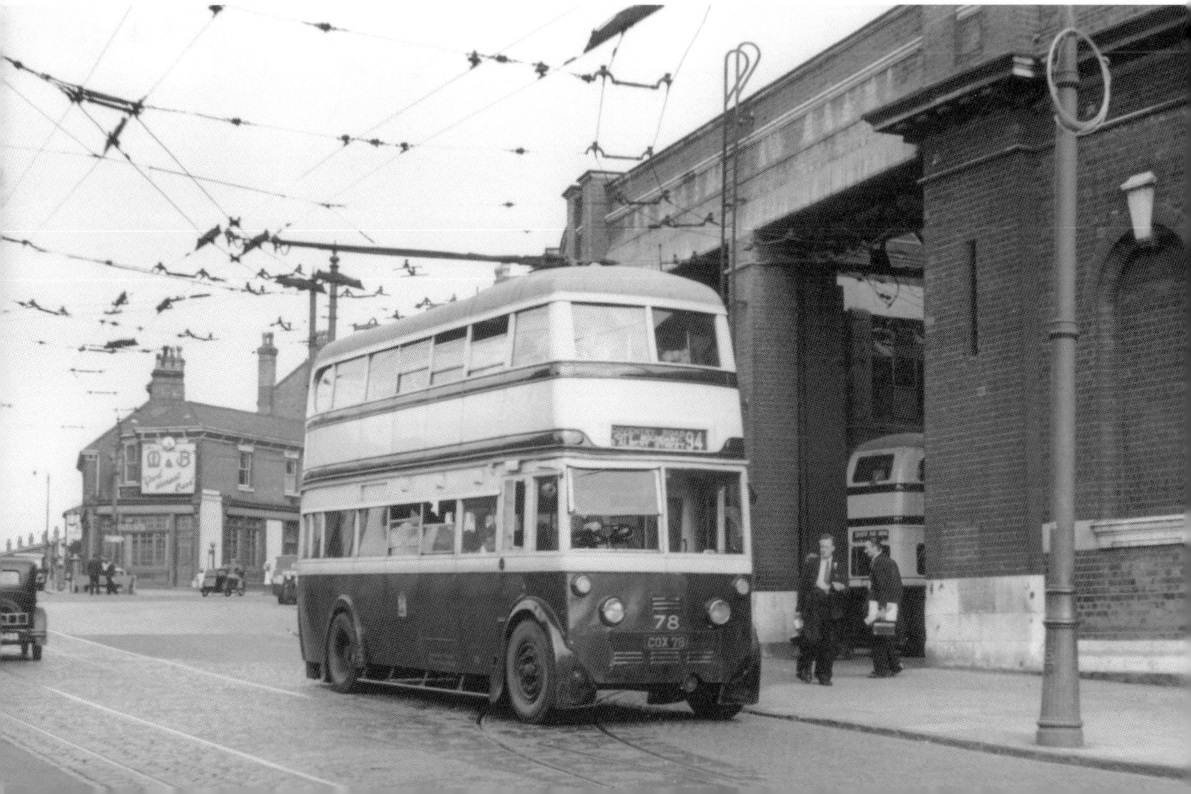
94
78

COVENTRY ROAD DEPOT

60.   Coventry Road/Arthur Street/depot/shed/garage, as it was variously known, had lost the Stechford route trams on 2nd October 1948. These were replaced by Daimler CVD6s, such as no. 1839 (HOV 839), which is about to leave on a 51 service to Belcher's Lane. Also at the depot

entrance on 13th June 1951 is Leyland TB5 trolleybus no. 75 (COX 75), which had first entered service on 22nd September 1937 and is about to take up a duty on a 94 turn. (G.F.Douglas/A.D.Packer)

61. Trolleybuses entering Coventry Road depot skirted around the eastern and southern sides of the interior, as is no. 89 (FOK 89) on the left beneath the offices, before lining up in usually six rows of either five or six trolleybuses in the centre of the depot. The rest of the 74 trolleybuses housed in the depot for the Coventry Road services were then parked around the perimeter. In the front of the three rows in the centre of the depot is one of each of the pre-war Leyland types with six wheeled trolleybus no. 22 (OC 1122) to the right, with TB5 no. 76 (COX 76) next to it and on the far side no. 82 (FOK 82), one of the 1940 TB7s. (J.S.Webb)

62.   On Sunday 3rd June 1951, the Omnibus Society undertook a visit to the Birmingham system using no. 90 (FOK 90) as their tour vehicle. Meanwhile back in Coventry Road depot, a slightly dented six wheeler no. 50 (OC 1150), a Leyland TTBD2 with Metro-Cammell H33/25R bodywork, stands alongside the six years younger Leyland TB7 no. 83 (FOK 83), with the offices behind the two vehicles. The MCCW body of no. 83 would survive with Silcox of Pembroke Dock until 1967 as ODE 402 on a Bristol K6G chassis. (R.Grosvenor)

63. On Sunday, 7th January 1934, trolleybuses took over from the tramcars on the Yardley services - 92 from Albert Street and 93 from Station Street. Sometime on the following day, trolleybus no. 25 (OC 1125) climbs up Kingston Hill, Coventry Road and passes the entrance to Coventry Road depot. Overhead is the complicated wiring necessary to gain access to and exit from the depot from all directions. Travelling down the hill is tramcar 130, which is working inbound on the 84 service from Bordesley Green. (Birmingham Post/Birmingham Central Reference Library)

64. Although trolleybuses ran a full service throughout the last day of operation, those which were not being used, such as 65 (OC 1165), were towed away even as other trolleybuses were maintaining the service. Looking a little dusty, this Leyland TTBD2 stands in Arthur Street behind one of W.T.Bird's AEC "Matadors", prior to being towed to Stratford for breaking up. A second "Matador" is making the turn into Arthur Street with another trolleybus in tow. (L.W.Perkins)

SMALL HEATH

65. On a miserable January day in 1934, brand new Leyland TTBD2 six-wheeler no. 28 (OC 1128) stands outside the Coventry Road depot entrance. The trolleybus is displaying the DEPOT ONLY destination and it appears from its position on the overhead that the trolleybus is about to turn into the depot. In the misty distance, the Coventry Road trolleybus wiring went to the right of the Greenaway Arms pub, while to the left is Cattell Road, used by the Stechford 84 tram route to Stechford. (D.R.Harvey coll.)

66. The overhead outside Coventry Road depot, with Herbert Road on the left, was the most complex on the BCT system as not only did it cater for normal service running, but also allowed both left and right turns in and out of the depot from either the City or the Small Heath side. The overhead junctions were all done manually by the conductors, as there were no automatic frogs on the Birmingham system. Out of sight in front of the pre-war Commer N1 20cwt van was a line of electric light bulbs which guided trolleybus drivers out of town to the right of the Greenaway Arms in foggy conditions. (D.R.Harvey coll.)

↗ 67. The light bulbs were to guide trolleybus drivers in foggy conditions. Leyland TTBD2 trolleybus no. 37 (OC 1137) is working on the normal 94 service to the City Boundary at Arden Oak Road, while in front of it is another of these six wheelers, no. 32 (OC 1132), which is on the 99 shortworking to Wagon Lane, introduced on 24th January 1949. On the rear platform are the stanchion poles covered with black Doverite, which reduced the possibility of getting an electric shock when boarding the trolleybus. (W.A.Camwell)

→ 68. Standing outside the shuttered frontage of L.G.Mills' greengrocers shop, just beyond Whitmore Road, is Leyland TB5 no. 67 (FOK 67). The trolleybus is travelling into the City on a rather deserted Sunday in June 1951 on a 94 service and has the trolleybus abandonment notices in the windows. Despite having only a matter of day's service left, the fourteen year old Metro-Cammell body looks in remarkably good condition. (R.Marshall)

BARBER
TEAS
PERSIL
washes whiter!
LOOKING FORWARD TO
94
37

LG MILLS
94
67
COX 67

69.   Pulling away from the Small Heath Congregational Church stop in March 1950 is trolleybus no. 72 (COX 72), a 1937 built Leyland TB5 with a MCCW H29/24R body. It is travelling out of the City and, once it has overtaken the Rover 14/6 saloon car, which is about two years older than the trolleybus, no. 72 will cross the Inner Circle 8 bus route at the Muntz Street junction. Opposite the trolleybus is the entrance to Langley Road. (D.Griffiths)

70.   Small Heath Park was opened on 5th April 1878 on a 44 acre site and was renamed Victoria Park, when the Queen visited on 23rd March 1887. In March 1950, with Charles Road in the distance, Leyland TB7 trolleybus no. 88 (FOK 88) is about to leave the stop outside Joan's costumier shop before beginning the descent of the hill towards Hay Mills. On the opposite side of the road, is the low retaining wall of the park. (D.Griffiths)

HAY MILLS

71. No. 67 (COX 67) is posed for an official photograph in wartime livery in the Hay Mills turning circle. This Leyland TB5 has received the necessary blackout alterations. The roof has been painted grey, the headlights have been masked and every bottom edge has been painted white, including the driver's cab step. (BCT)

72. About to leave the utility passenger shelter on 2nd May 1950 is Metro-Cammell-bodied trolleybus no. 25 (OC 1125). It is on a 93 working to Albert Street and is opposite the billboard festooned booking office of Eatonways Coaches. Behind the trolleybus and through the stanchions of the shelter is the Bundy Clock in the Hay Mills turning circle, while on the right beyond the River Cole bridge, looking towards Yardley, is the Plough & Harrow public house.
(G.F.Douglas/A.D.Packer)

→ 73. Four wheel trolleybus no. 73 (COX 73) stands on the cobbled section of roadway in Coventry Road with the Hay Mills turning circle behind it. This loop was used as the terminus for the shortworking 56 service from Albert Street and the 57 service from Station Street. This 53 seater Leyland TB5, which entered service on 18th September 1937, is working on the 94 service to the City Boundary at Sheldon in 1951. Over the penultimate offside lower saloon window is the panelled-over destination box, which was made redundant during the war in an attempt to save destination blind linen.
(S.N.J.White)

↓ 74. It is Wednesday, 28th March 1951, as two Leyland TTBD2 trolleybuses, led by no. 21 (OC 1121), stand at the Hay Mills stop adjacent to the trolleybus turning circle. It is working on the 96 service from Albert Street to the Rover Works in Lode Lane, Solihull, which was the least employed of the normal Coventry Road services. Parked in the turning circle, no. 38 (OC 1138) is being used for learner driver duty, which is slightly surprising in view of the imminent abandonment. (G.F.Douglas/A.D.Packer)

75. The inspector has opened the nearside cab door in order to talk to the driver of trolleybus 58 (OC 1158), as it waits alongside the Bundy Clock at the Hay Mills turning loop in Coventry Road. The trolleybus is working on the 99 route to Wagon Lane in 1951 and drawn up behind 58 is another six-wheel Leyland working on the full distance 94 service to the city boundary. (T.Barker)

THE SWAN

76. Standing next to Arthur Hemming's builders' merchant yard on Saturday, 3rd June 1950 is no. 32 (OC 1132). The trolleybus is at the Church Road stop opposite the Yardley trolleybus terminus and is working on the "mainline" 94 service. The first of the Victorian built premises belonged to George Davies and was a saddlery shop. (J.H.Meredith)

77. Leaving the trolleybus stop and about to negotiate the complicated overhead as it approaches the Coventry Road/Church Road traffic island, is a Sheldon-bound trolleybus, Leyland TB5 no. 71 with a MCCW body. Behind the trolleybus is an early postwar British Road Services ERF articulated lorry leading a row of vehicles up the steep hill from Hay Mills. (C.Martin)

→ 78. Birmingham's method of collecting the 550 Volts DC current from the overhead was by trolleywheels, whose "swishing" noise would be heard well in advance of the arrival of the trolleybus. The trolleybus is no. 80 (FOK 80), one of the 1940 batch of Leyland TB7s. It is passing Tonks' grocery and confectioners shop on 6th June 1949. To the left of the trolleybus is the curving overhead, which took the original 92 and 93 trolleybus services into the Yardley trolleybus station. (G.F. Douglas/A.D. Packer)

→ 79. A 1934 registered Austin 7 trundles out of Yardley Road and begins to cross Coventry Road at the Swan junction. A pair of eighteen month old Leyland TTBD2s stand in the original Yardley terminus turning circle on Friday, 26th June 1935. The rear trolleybus is no. 53 (OC 1153), which is working on the 93 service to Albert Street. After July 1936, a new entrance to the Yardley trolleybus turning circle was made where the impressive bus shelter for the Outer Circle buses is located, in order for inbound trolleybuses to get into the former terminus.
(Birmingham Central Reference Library)

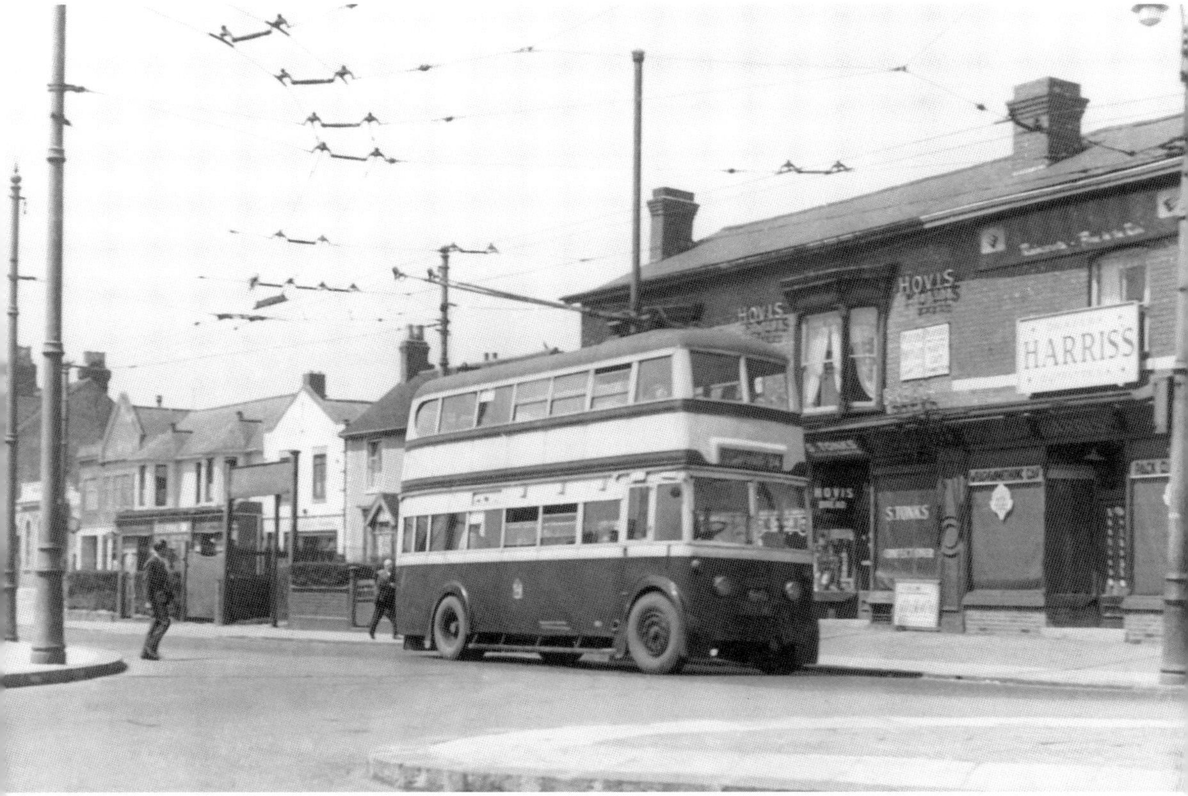
HOVIS
HOVIS
HARRISS
S. TONKS

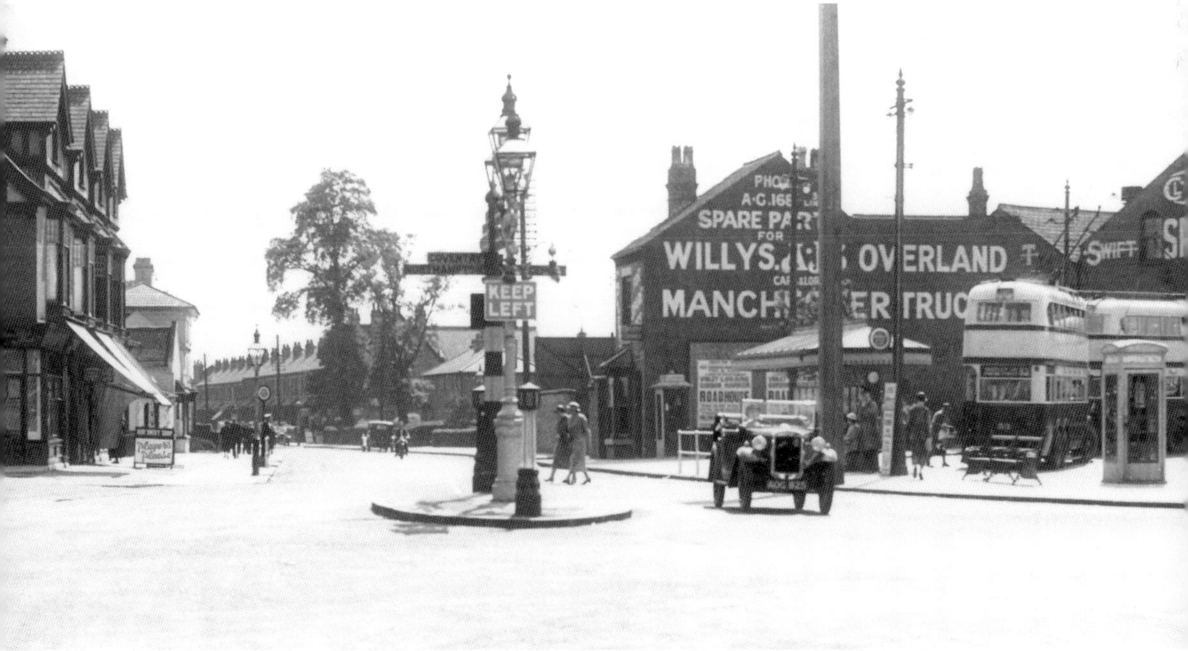
KEEP
LEFT
OVERLAND
SWIFT

80. Once the extension to the City Boundary at Arden Oak Road, Sheldon was opened on 5th July 1936, the arrangement at the former Yardley terminus was altered to allow the trolleybuses to come in from Sheldon. These trolleybuses used the left hand pair of wires as the right hand ones formed the end of the loop for the 92 and 93 route shortworkings. Standing at the impressive green painted shelters is six-wheeled Leyland no. 43 (OC 1143). The sign NO ENTRY TROLLEY BUSES ONLY was unique on the system. (G.F.Douglas)

→ 81. Parked in the Yardley terminus loop is the almost new MCCW bodied Leyland TTBD2 no. 59 (OC1159), which is working on the 92 route to Albert Street on 5th September 1934. Behind the still pristine trolleybus is the Swan public house on the far side of Yardley Road. Next to the shelter behind the trolleybus is the Bundy clocking-in timepiece. (D.R.Harvey coll.)

→ 82. The 24th May 1951 was a sunny spring day and at the Yardley trolleybus station, three trolleybuses bask in the bright sunshine. On the right is no. 42 (OC 1142), a 1934 Leyland TTBD2 with an MCCW body, whose driver is climbing into the cab through the nearside cab door. These six wheelers were some of the last vehicles delivered to BCT without the deep cream painted waistrail. Parked next to it on the shortworking overhead is four wheeler no. 75 (COX 75), which will shortly depart for Station Street. (G.F.Douglas)

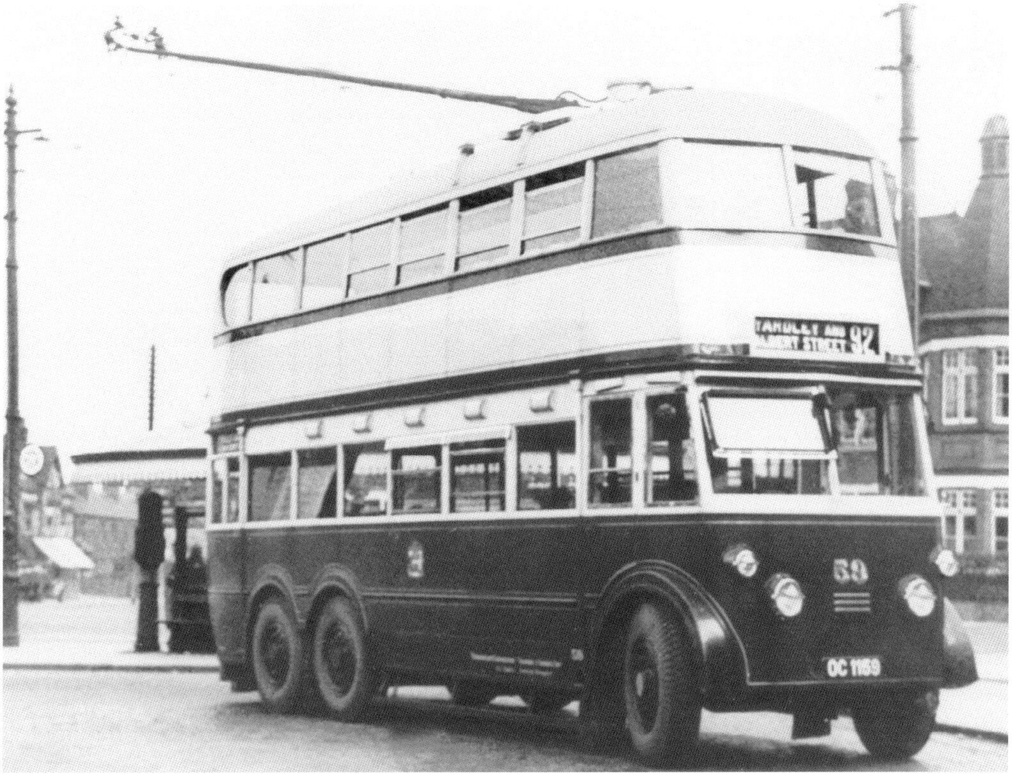
92
OC 1159

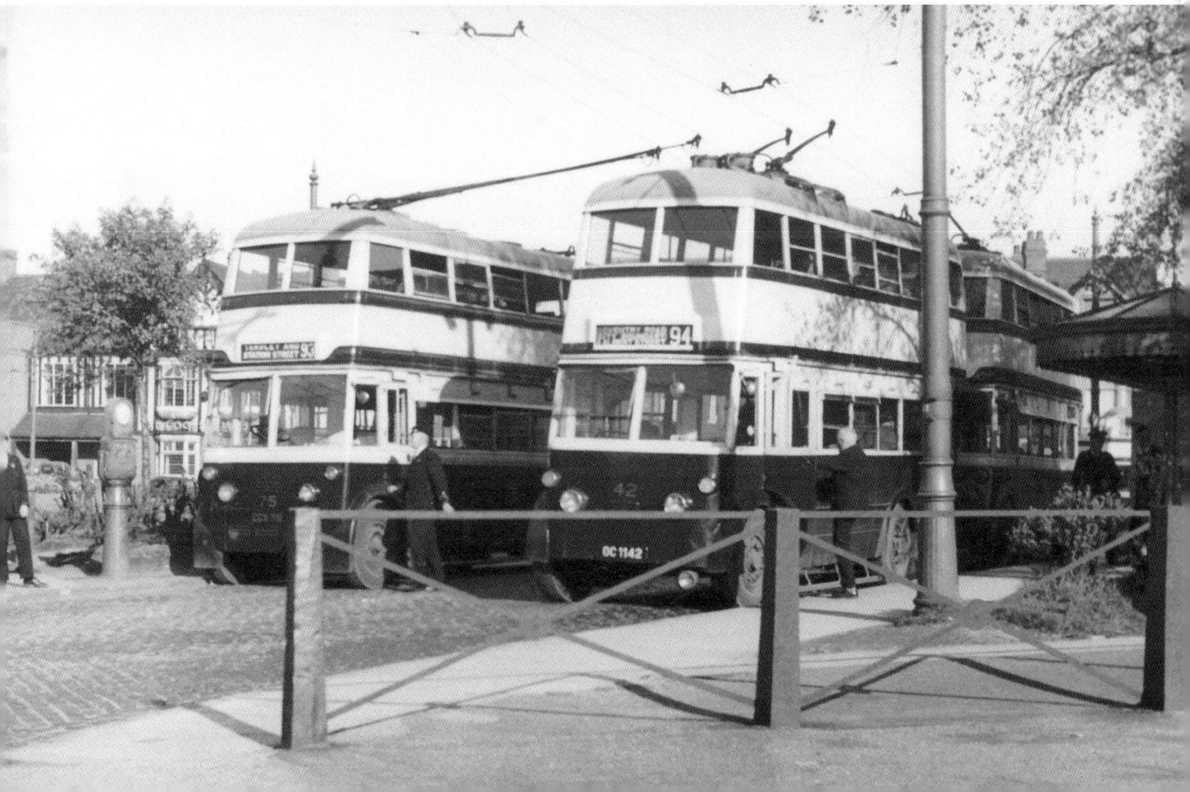
94
42
OC 1142

83. Standing in the Yardley trolleybus station in the shadow of the two large trees is trolleybus no. 82 (FOK 82). This 54 seater is working on the 94 route which is why it is parked alongside the substantial passenger shelter and just short of the Bundy Clock on the outside of the large turning loop. This Leyland TB7 trolleybus is seen during the last week of the Coventry Road trolleybus service, as the abandonment notices are posted in the lower saloon windows. Behind the passenger shelter on the right is the showroom of R.H.Collier, which was known as Collier's Corner and was housed in the former CBT Yardley tram depot, which closed in 1913. (R.Wilson)

↙ 84. Turning back into the Yardley trolleybus loop is Leyland TB5 four wheeler no. 69 (COX 69). The empty trolleybus is working on the 92 service back to Albert Street. The conductress standing on the back platform and wearing the optional, and for the time, slightly 'racy' slacks, is holding on to the platform stanchion. Above the trolleybus are the two sets of inbound trolleybus wires and a set of fog marker light bulbs, while behind the traction pole on the left is The Swan public house. (J.H.Meredith)

SOUTH YARDLEY

85. The 1936 extension from The Swan, Yardley to Sheldon added another 2.51 miles to the original 5.23 mile route and reflected the rapid urban growth in the South Yardley and Sheldon areas during the late 1930s. Leaving the stop at Charles Edward Road, which was the last inbound stop before the Swan, is trolleybus no. 35 (OC 1135), working City bound on the 94 route. Overtaking this MCCW bodied Leyland TTBD2 trolleybus is an early Morris Eight saloon. The mock half timbered building is the Butlers owned New Inn which was well known for its bowling green, but was pulled down in 1968. (R.Wilson)

86. From just beyond the Good Companions public house, on the corner of Steyning Road, and to beyond Gilbertstone Avenue, the mid 1930s detached housing was built well back from Coventry Road with separate service roads on each side. MCCW bodied Leyland TTBD2 no. 29 (OC 1129) is working on the 94 service in June 1951. (R.Wilson)

→ 87. Having ascended the hill on the one way New Coventry Road from Lyndon End, trolleybus 58 (OC 1158) joins the wide two way Coventry Road at Brays Road in the last year of trolleybus operation. The trolleybus is working inbound to the City terminus in Albert Street. This road had been constructed immediately prior to the extension of the trolleybuses from Yardley to the City Boundary in Sheldon. The original part of Coventry Road is to the left of the property development sign. (R.Wilson)

→ 88. At the bottom of the hill beyond Brays Road was Lyndon End, a collection of Georgian and Victorian cottages scattered around the Coventry Road junction with Wagon Lane and Barrows Lane. At this junction was the large roadside Wagon & Horses public house, which in 1938 had replaced a much smaller mainly Victorian hostelry, which incorporated a part dating from 1627. Leyland six-wheeler no. 32 (OC 1132) speeds down the hill on a 94 service towards the Arden Oak Road terminus. (R.Wilson)

JACK COTTON

THIS
SOLD
SITE
JACK COTTON
& PARTNERS
BIRMINGHAM

SHELDON

89. A distant view of the one way system in Coventry Road has the Wagon & Horses and the Rondelle garage on the extreme left. The vehicle unloading at the stop at Lyndon End is no. 62 (OC 1162). This Leyland TTBD2 six wheeler with a 58 seat Metro-Cammell body is working on the 94 service to Sheldon. On the right is the Lyndon End Recreation ground with Wesley Brook flowing through the open parkland. (R.Wilson)

→ 90. The last modification to the Birmingham trolleybus system occurred on 24th January 1949, when a turn back loop was put in to enable trolleybuses to turn right from Coventry Road into New Coventry Road and return towards the City. This new shortworking was numbered 99 and was introduced so that fewer trolleybuses had to queue in Coventry Road just before the Arden Oak Road terminus. The angle of the turn was sufficiently tight that the wires into New Coventry Road had to take a much wider turn. Leyland TTBD2 trolleybus no. 21 (OC 1121) is undertaking this manoeuvre on 23rd April 1951. In the background is dewired six-wheeler no. 66 (OC 1166), which is being attended to by one of the Corporation's AEC "Mercury" tower wagons. (G.F.Douglas/A.D.Packer)

→ 91. Passing the 1930s semi-detached houses, which lined New Coventry Road at Lyndon End, is trolleybuses no. 29 (OC 1129). The trolleybus is travelling into the City on the 94 service in early 1949 and is approaching the junction with Wagon Lane. Its trolleypoles have just cleared the point where the Wagon Lane turn back overhead rejoins the mainline. (Birmingham City Transport)

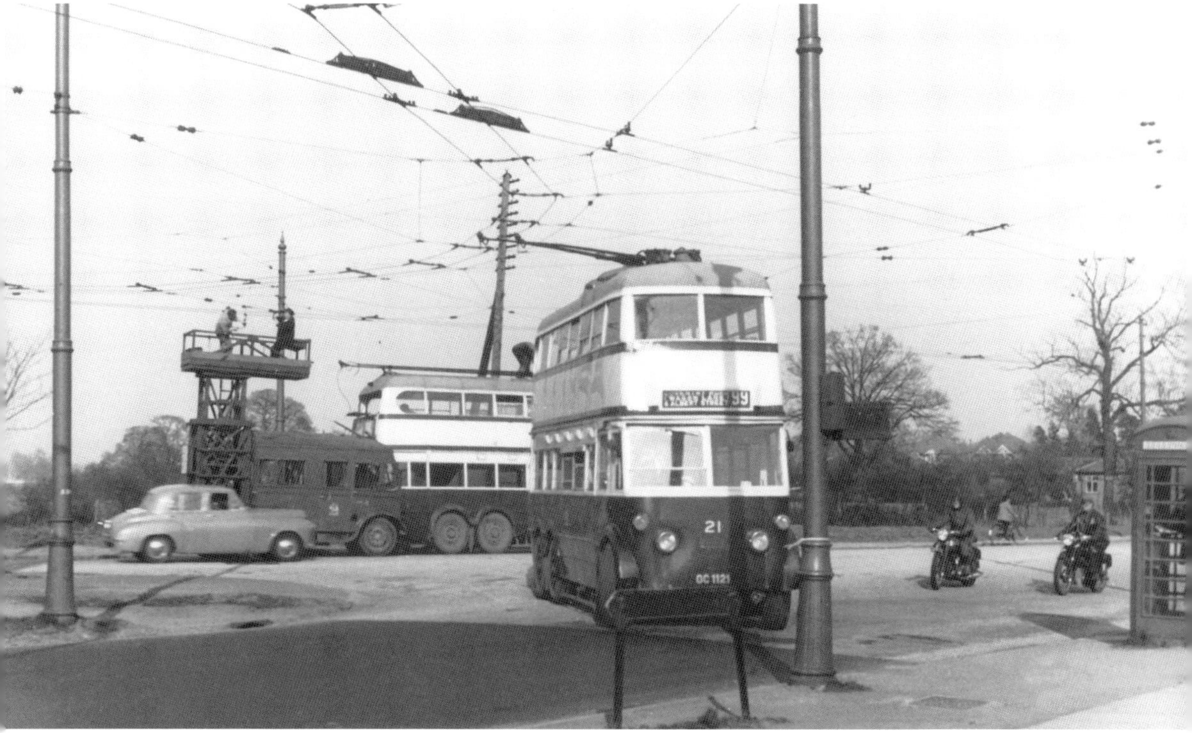
21
DC 1121

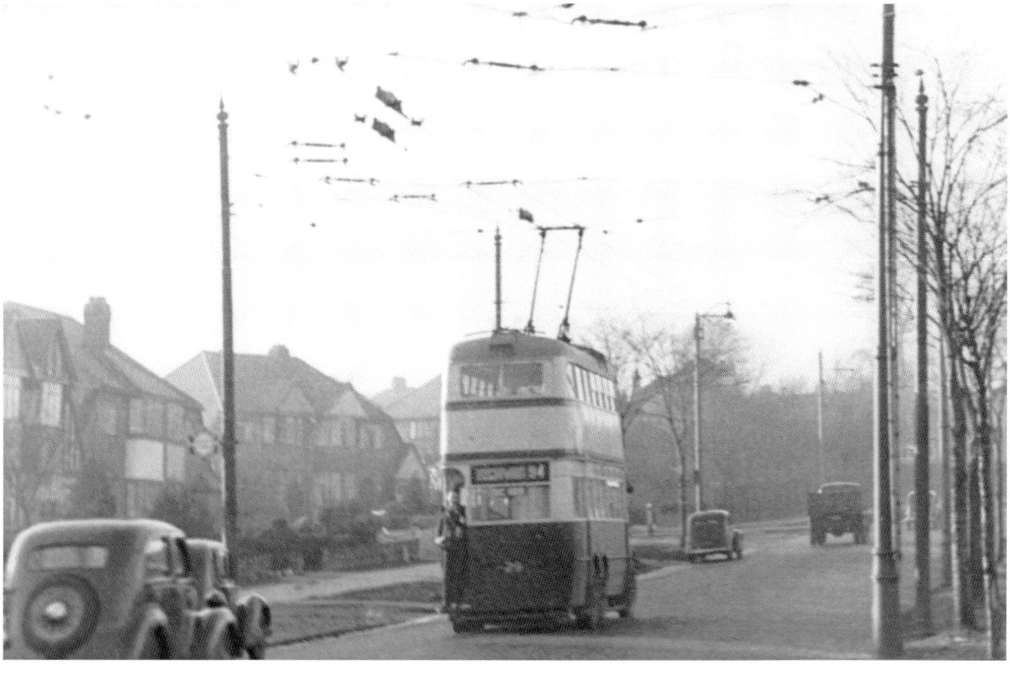

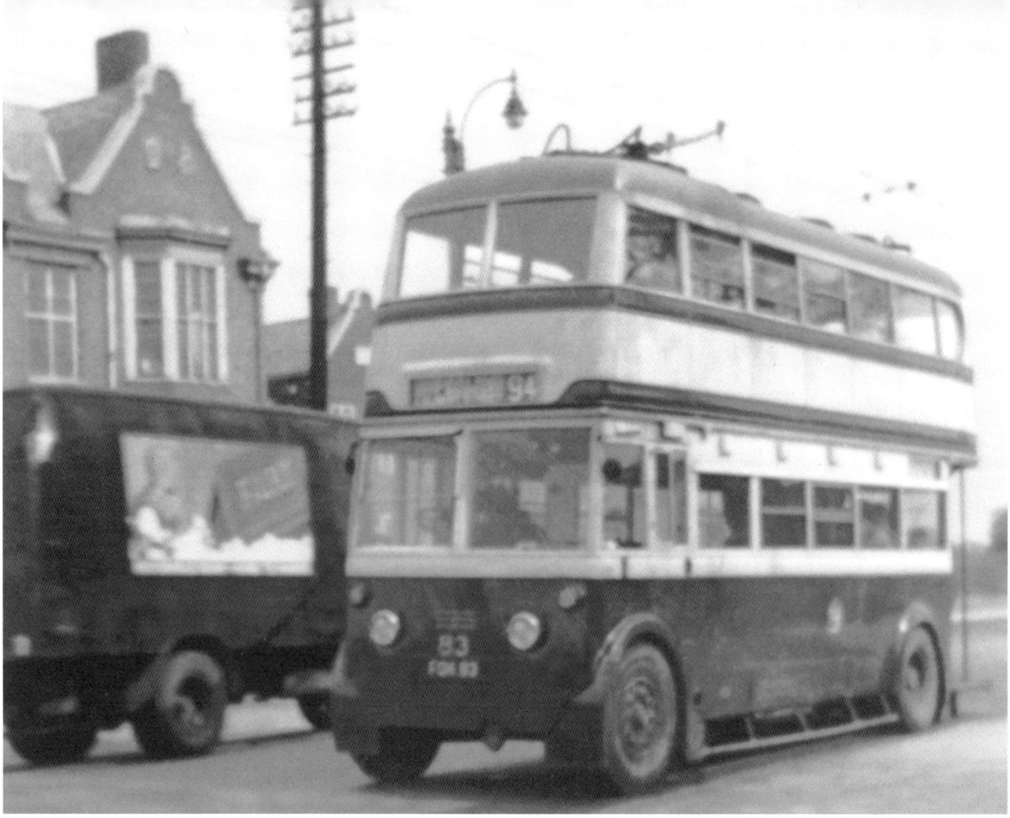

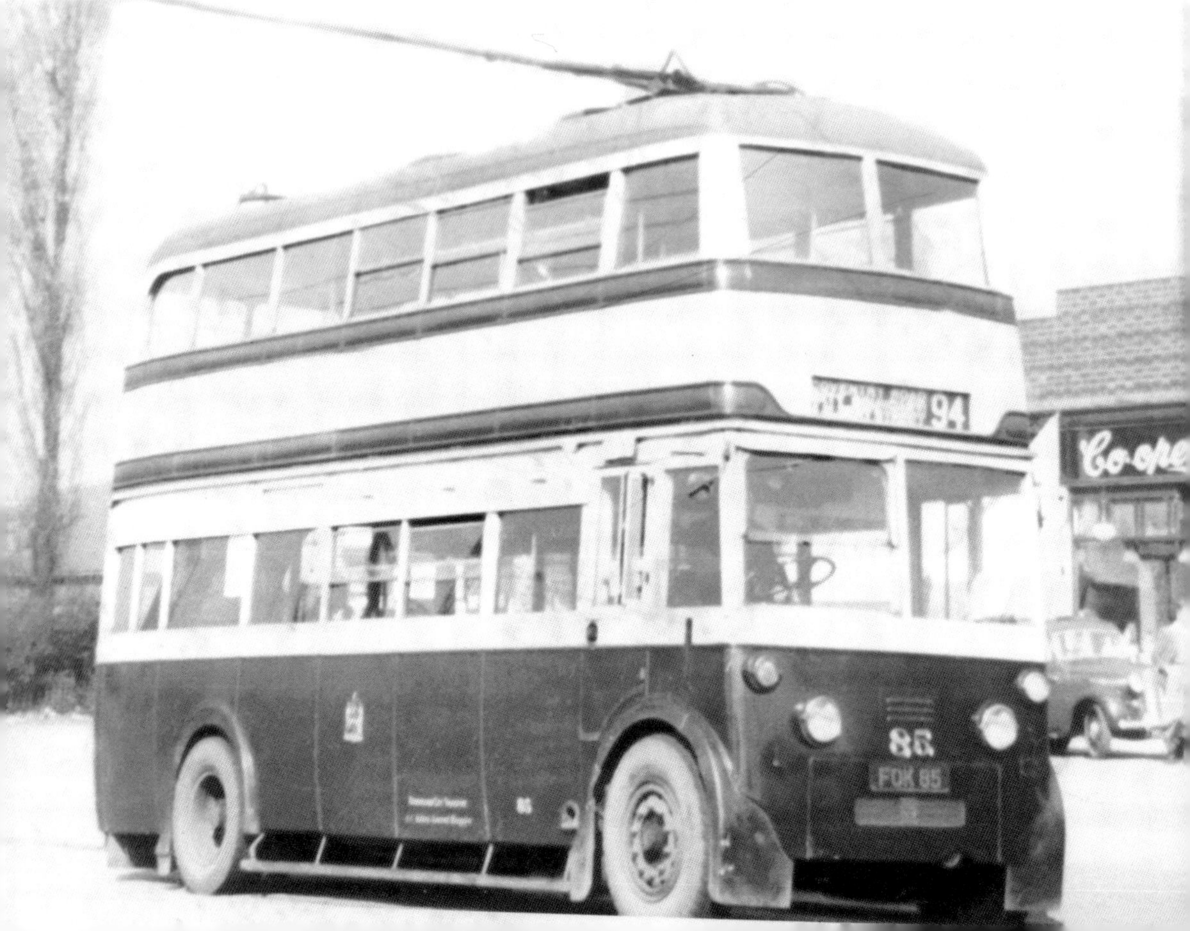
94
FOK 85

← 92. Having pulled away from the inbound stop at the Wheatsheaf, another Leyland TB7 trolleybus, this time no. 83 (FOK 83), accelerates past the large, Dutch gabled, Edwardian Three Horse Shoes public house on its way into the City on the 94 route. These 1940 built Metro-Cammell vehicles could be distinguished from the previous COX registered batch of twelve by their lack of guttering over the upper saloon front windows. (D.Griffiths)

← 93. The last trolleybus stop in Coventry Road before the right turn into Hobs Moat Road was outside the Sheldon branch of the Birmingham Co-operative grocery and provisions shop. About to pull away from the stop on the 94 service is no. 85 (FOK 85), one of the 1940 batch of GEC 80 hp motored Leyland TB7s. Although having traction batteries like the COX registered batch, these Metro-Cammell bodied trolleybuses had 54 seats and were among the last vehicles to receive the standard BCT pre-war body style. (D.Griffiths)

94. A fairly large number of people stand in a queue at the stop next to the Wheatsheaf public house. On 23rd April 1951, Leyland TB7 trolleybus 80 (FOK 80) is being loaded up with the help of the conductor when working on the 94 service to Albert Street. (G.F.Douglas/A.D.Packer)

95. Standing outside the forecourt of the Wheatsheaf public house on 11th June 1950 is a very smart looking trolleybus, no. 40 (OC 1140), one of the fifty 1934 built Leyland TTBD2s fitted with an MCCW H33/25R body. This trolleybus amassed some 521,010 miles during its seventeen year service life. Between the pub sign and the trolleybus is one of the totally inadequate wartime tubular steel bus shelters. Behind the pub sign is the trolleybus overhead leading into Hobs Moat Road with Shakespeare's newsagents shop on the corner, while 1½ miles beyond is the Rover car factory in Lode Lane. (G.F.Douglas/A.D.Packer)

→ 96. The half mile stretch from the Wheatsheaf to the terminus at Arden Oak Road was typical "trolleybus suburbia", being flat, virtually straight, with ribbon development of semi-detached houses set back from the wide and originally concrete slabbed road surface. Trolleybus no. 43 (OC 1143), one of the Leyland TTBD2s which had opened the Coventry Road service in January 1934, has left the distant terminus and is running empty back to Coventry Road depot displaying DEPOT ONLY rather than the allotted 98 service. This number was available for passenger carrying duties between the same points. (H.Harcourt/Birmingham Central Reference Library Local Studies)

→ 97. About to disgorge its passengers at the compulsory Stop sign opposite Wells Road is another one of the Leyland six wheelers. They were popular on the "mainline" 94 service and on the Lode Lane routes to the Rover Works, because they could seat four or five more than the newer four wheelers and squeeze in at least another eight standing! No. 25 (OC 1125) will move off to join the queue of trolleybuses waiting in Coventry Road prior to taking up their turn at the Arden Oak terminus. (S.E.Letts)

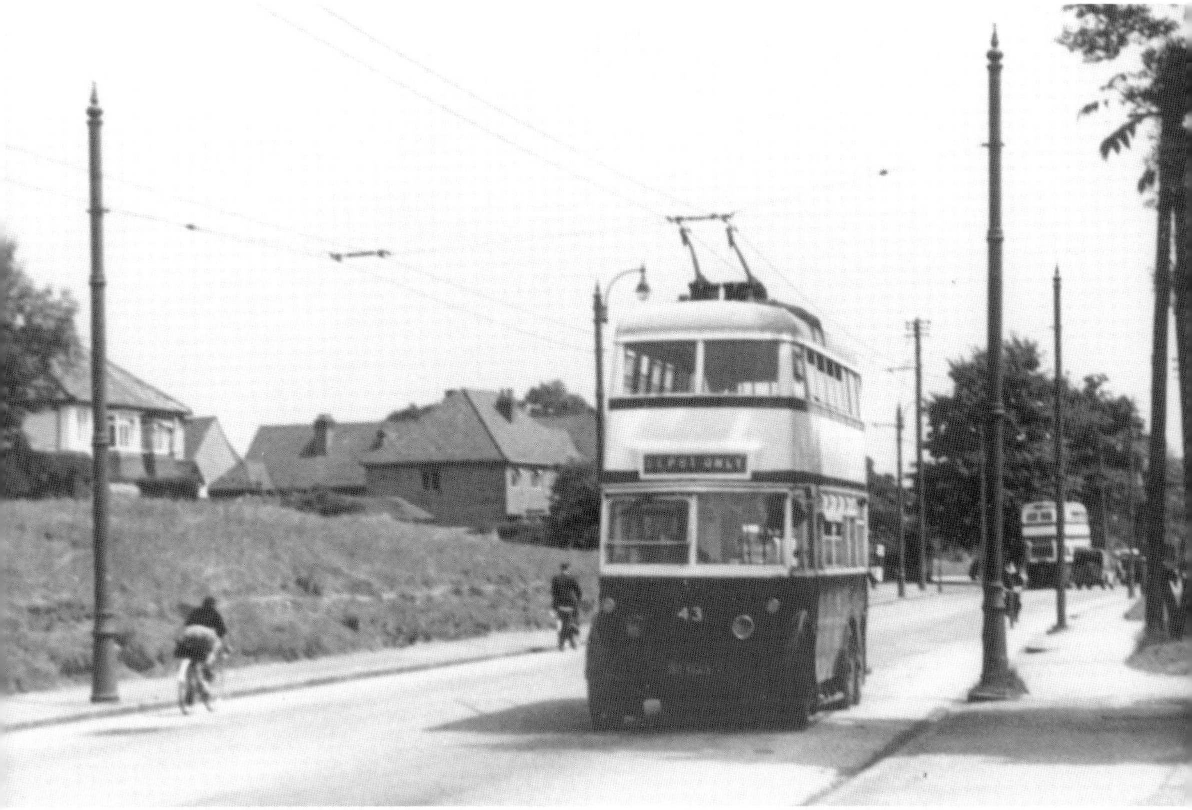
43

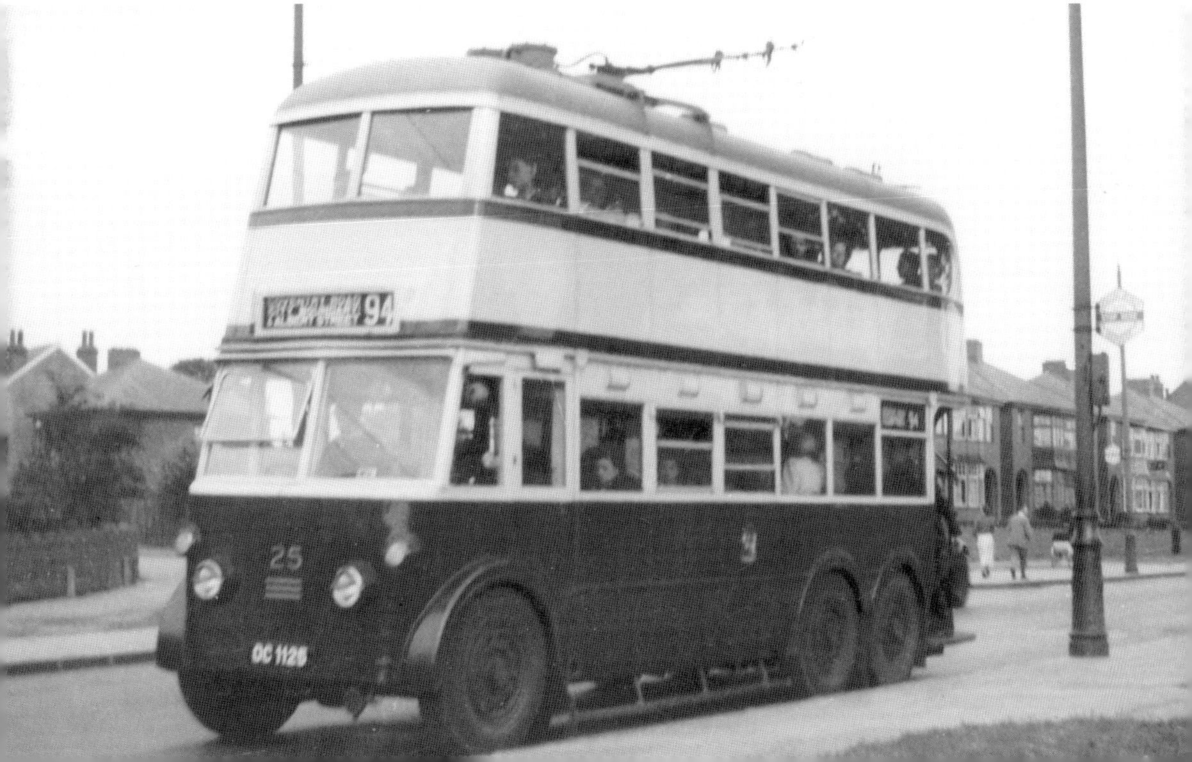
94
25

98. This is what happened everyday near to the 94 route terminus. Trolleybuses arriving from the City had to park nose-to-tail in Coventry Road, as they waited their turn to enter the Arden Oak turning circle. There the driver pegged the Bundy Clock at their allotted departure time and then swung across the main A45 carriageway as they began their 7 mile 1,221 yard journey back to the City Centre. Two Metro-Cammell bodied Leyland four wheelers, 73 (COX 73) of 1937 and 82 (FOK 82) of 1940, stand waiting for the trolleybus in front to leave the terminus. (D.Griffiths)

→ 99. Sunday, 11th June 1950 was obviously a warm sunny day with the man snoozing in the sunshine on the bench. The trolleybus driver, who is about to "peg" the Bundy Clock, is in his shirt sleeves and all the trolleybus windows are open. The trolleybus terminus at Arden Oak Road served the 1930s built Cranes Park Estate and a row of shops was developed near to the turning circle. To the left of trolleybus 32 (OC 1132) is a Wrensons grocery and provisions store and a Wimbush bread and cake shop, whose bakery was in Green Lane, Small Heath. (G.F.Douglas/A.D.Packer)

→ 100. The terminus at Arden Oak Road in the days of trolleybuses really marked the edge of the City. Next to the bushes on the right was a group of willow trees and beyond that was open countryside and the nearby Hatchford Brook, a tributary of the River Cole. The City boundary was 0.4 miles away at Tiger's Island. Powers had been obtained to operate to this point, but there was no suitable turning place, although there was a 40 yard length of overhead which was used for overhead electrical power supplies. Standing at the terminus is six-wheeler no. 20 (OC 1120) with the abandonment notices in its windows. (Stratford Guild Library)

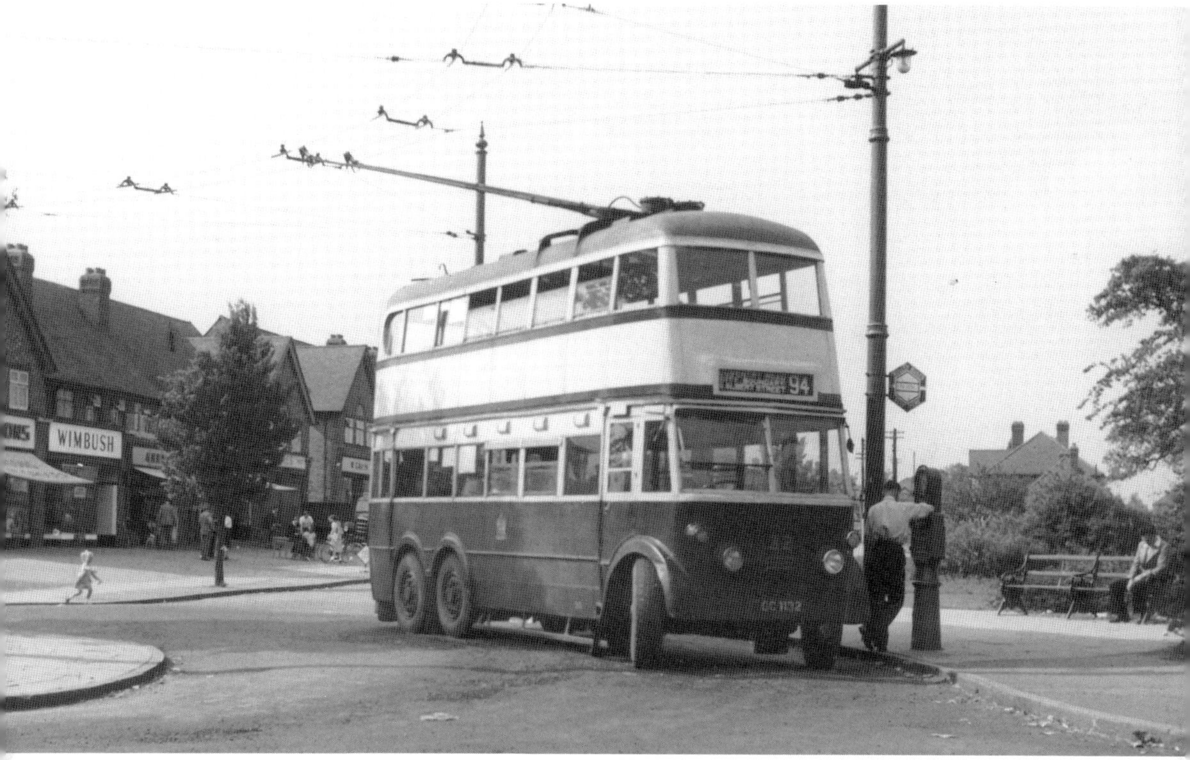
WIMBUSH
94

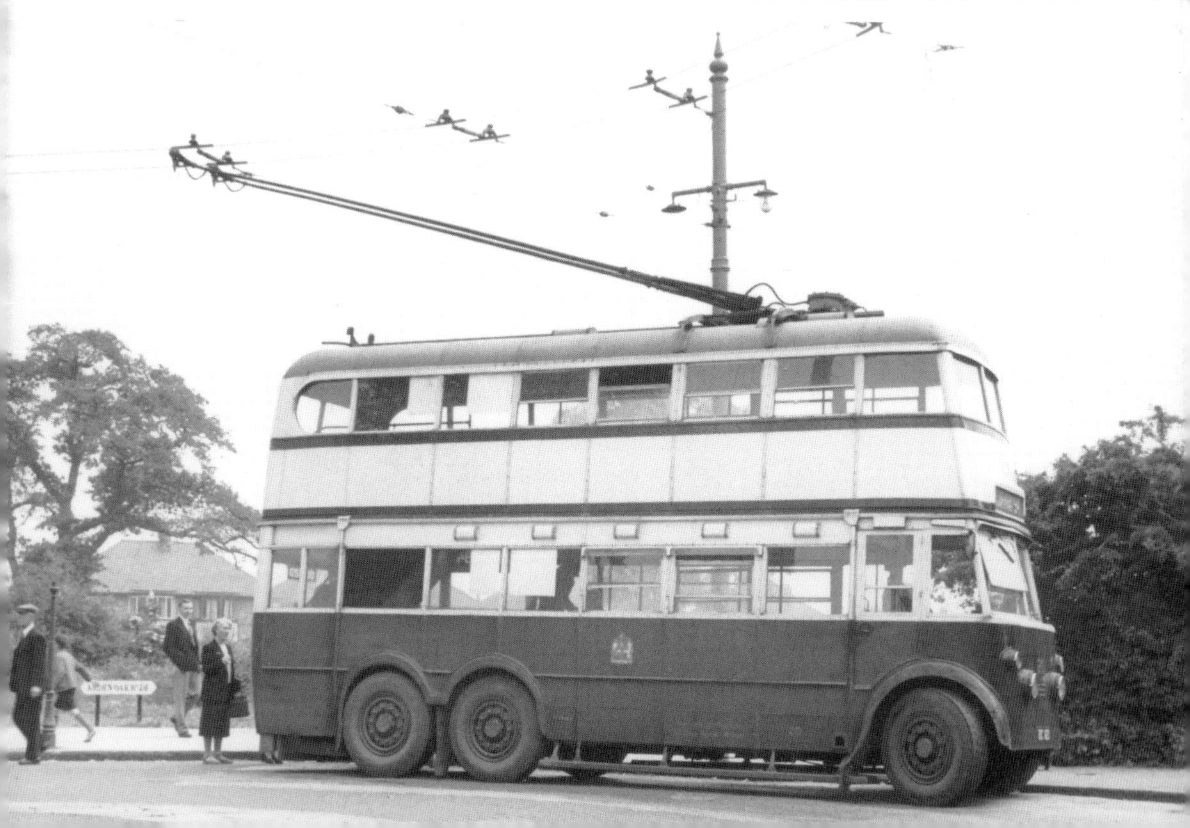

101. In the summer of 1950, trolleybus no. 68 (COX 68), a Leyland TB5 with a Metro-Cammell H29/24R body, stands alongside the Bundy Clock in the turning loop at Arden Oak Road. The trolleybus is shortly due to leave on the long journey back to Albert Street. On the corner of Arden Oak Road is the converted caravan which was used for a number of years as a tea bar by the trolleybus crews. (D.Barlow)

102. GEC 65 hp powered Leyland TTBD2 no. 59 (OC 1159) has just left the terminus where the Standard 8 car is about to pass the Bundy Clock. Beyond the trolleybus is the bridge over Hatchford Brook and the tied off 40 yard stretch of overhead wire. As part of the Birmingham Corporation Act of 1935 which was the legislation to extend the Coventry Road route from Yardley to the boundary, a proposal was made to take the trolleybuses to the Tiger's Island boundary and if successful, perhaps the trolleybus route might have been extended for a second time to Elmdon Airport. (D.W.K.Jones)

LODE LANE

103. The Lode Lane branch turned right at the Wheatsheaf into Hobs Moat Road where the trolleybuses pulled up at the stop outside Shakespeare's newsagents shop. Leyland TTBD2 six-wheeler no. 42 (OC 1142) is working on the less common 96 service from Albert Street. The 1½ mile long service to the Rover Works in Solihull was introduced on 29th October 1941 under the Emergency Powers (Defence) Parliamentary Act of 1939. This was to conserve fuel and led to the Corporation's trolleybuses operating deep into Midland Red's territory. (W.A.Camwell)

104. On Friday, 29th July 1951, the penultimate day of Birmingham's trolleybus operation, nearly empty trolleybus no. 45 (OC 1145) closes the Lode Lane branch with just a whizzing noise coming from its trolleyhead wheels. Late on the following day this seventeen year old Leyland would become the last passenger carrying trolleybus to operate on the 94 service. The semi-rural nature of Hobs Moat Road is noteworthy, though in the distance suburbia's march can be seen encroaching across the fields. (G.B.Claydon)

105. The driver of Leyland TB5 waits to come out of the Rover Works on 23rd April 1951, having failed to change the front destination from showing 94 to the correct 96. Although the Metro-Cammell bodies on the 1937 and 1940 built Leyland four wheel trolleybuses were similar to the contemporary motorbuses, the body pillars on either side of the first bay in each saloon were noticeably wider as they carried the power cables from the trolleypoles to the traction motors. (G.F.Douglas/A.D.Packer)

→ 106. As the workers leave the Rover factory at the end of their shift, Leyland six wheeled Metro-Cammell bodied trolleybus no. 20 (OC 1120) stands at the factory terminus in Valiant Way. It is outside the original camouflaged brick built shadow factory, which was only completed in late 1939. The trolleybus is being employed on the 96 service while behind it is no. 26 (OC 1126) and in the distance four wheeled no. 77 (COX 77). (W.A.Camwell)

107. The first of the two farewell tours of the Birmingham system took place on 3rd June 1951 and was organised by the Omnibus Society. They used Leyland TB7 no. 90 (FOK 90). This trolleybus entered service on 20th February 1940 and had the distinction of being used on both tours, as well as being the vehicle to close the system. It is standing outside the original buildings and is displaying the 97 route destination to Station Street. (R.Grosvenor)

ROLLING STOCK

108. The top deck of the body is covered with a tarpaulin, as Railless no. 11 (OK 4833) awaits a tow behind the National Transport's Leyland articulated lorry to Birmingham, where it arrived just three days before the opening of the Nechells trolleybus service. The bodybuilding contract had been subcontracted by Railless and effectively bankrupted Charles H.Roe as the Receiver was brought in during September 1922, while the construction of these twelve trolleybuses was underway. (D.R.Harvey coll.)

109. The batch of three Railless LF trolleybuses numbered 14-16 (ON 2825-2827) all entered service in March 1926 and had fairly brief lives, as they were taken out of service in 1932, when replacement trolleybuses entered service. By this time the union between Railless and Short Brothers had been established for about a year and so these solid tyred tracklesses were bodied "in-house" by Shorts. One of the batch stands on the forecourt of Washwood Heath depot trailing a skate for access to the route, while tram no. 787 is just inside the car shed.
(Birmingham City Transport)

TROLLEYBUS FLEET

1-12, OK 4823-4834.
Railless F12 chassis. 2x42hp DK 85A series-wound motors. EEC Form D hand-controller. Roe H25/26RO bodies. Entered service 27/10/1922-24/11/1924. Withdrawn 2/1932-8/1932.

13, OL 993.
AEC 602 chassis. 2x42 BTH GE247A series-wound motors. BTH hand-controller. Brush B36R body. AEC, Southall demonstrator 17/8/23-10/23. Sold to Mexborough & Swinton, 31.

13, OL 4636.
EMB chassis. 2x42 DK 85A series-wound motors. EEC Form D hand-controller. Roe H28/20R body. EMB, Wednesbury demonstrator 4/1924-21/4/1926.

00, TO 5011.
Railless LF chassis. 2x35hp DK 99A series-wound motors. EEC Form D foot-controller. Short H26/26RO body. 1925 CMS exhibit in BCT livery, but rejected. To Nottingham CT, 10.

14-16, ON 2825-2827.
Railless LF chassis. 2x 35hp DK 99A series-wound motors. EEC Form D hand-controller. Short H25/26RO body. Es 3/1926. W. 2/1932-8/1932.

17, ON 3261.
AEC 607 chassis. 1x55hp Bull series-wound motor. EMB foot-controller. Vickers H26/26RO body. AEC, Southall demonstrator 3/1926. Purchased -/1926. W.8/1932.

18, UK 8341.
Guy BTX chassis. 1x60hp Rees-Roturbo compound-wound motor. Rees-Stevens controller. Guy H27/26R. 22/2/1930-31/5/1931. To Llanelli & District 17, 1/1935.

19, OG 9886.
Guy BTX chassis. 1x75hp Rees-Roturbo compound-wound motor. Rees-Stevens controller. Guy H27/26R, (straight staircase). Guy Motors, Wolverhampton demonstrator 4/1931-4/1931. To Llanelli & District 16, 1/1935.

19, OV 1175.
Leyland TBD1 chassis. 1x65hp GEC WT 265 series-wound motor. GEC FA3B controller. Leyland L24/24R half-cab body. Leyland Motors, Leyland demonstrator 5/1931-8/1931. Converted to TD1 petrol-engined motorbus and to Jersey MT as 24, J 1199, 2/1934. Preserved since 1958.

20, OV 1194.
Guy BT chassis. 1x60hp Rees-Roturbo compound-wound motor. Rees-Stevens controller. Park Royal L24/24R body. Guy Motors, Wolverhampton demonstrator 5/1931-5/1931. Converted to FC petrol-engined motorbus and to Truman, Shirebrook, -/1934.

1-3/5-7/9-11/13/15, OV 4001-3/5-7/9-11/13/15.
Leyland TBD1 chassis. 1x65hp GEC WT 251 series-wound motor. GEC FA3B controller. Short H27/21R half-cab body. Es.2/1932. W.2/1940-9/1940.

00, 0000.
AEC 663T chassis. 1x80hp EE DK 130F motor. EE controller. EEC H33/27R body Built 5/1930. Exhibited at 1931 CMS with EEC H31/24D body. AEC, Southall demonstrator 28/6/1932. Chassis renumbered and rebuilt and to BCT as 16, (OJ 1016).

12-16, OJ 1012-1016.
AEC 663T chassis. 1x80hp EE DK 130F motor. EE controller. Brush H33/25R. Es.8/1932-9/1932. W.9/1940.

87, RD 8085.
Sunbeam MF2A chassis. 1x80hp BTH 202 compound-wound motor. BTH controllers. Park Royal L24/24R body. Exhibited at 1933 CMS in BCT livery; never delivered to BCT. To Reading CT 1, RD 8085 3/1936.

17, TJ 939.
Leyland TTBD1 chassis. 1x65hp GEC WT 257 series-wound motor. GEC FA3A controller. Leyland H34/26R body. Leyland Motors, Leyland demonstrator 3/1933-7/1933.

17-66, OC 1117-1166.
Leyland TTBD2 chassis. 1x65 GEC WT 254c series-wound motor. GEC FA3B controller. MCCW H33/25R body, (contract 36). Es.1/1934-13/1934. W.2/1951-6/1951.

67, OC 6567.
Sunbeam MS2 chassis. 1x80hp BTH 201BY compound-wound motor. BTH controller.
MCCW H31/28R body, (contract 24). Sunbeam Motors, Wolverhampton demonstrator 2/1934-3/1934. To Wolverhampton CT, 222, 9/1934.

68, TJ 939.
Leyland TTBD1 chassis. 1x65hp GEC WT 254c series-wound motor. GEC FA3A controller. Leyland H34/26R body. Re-motored ex-BCT 17. Leyland Motors, Leyland demonstrator 7/1936-9/1937.

67-78, COX 67-78.
Leyland TB5 chassis. 1x80hp GEC WT2516J series-wound motor. GEC FA3A controller. Fitted with traction batteries. Es.9/1937-10/1937. W.6/1951.

79-90, FOK 79-90.
Leyland TB7 chassis. 1x80hp GEC WT2516P series wound motor. GEC FA3A controller. Fitted with traction batteries. Es 1/1940-2/1940. W.5/1951-6/1951.

110. The last of the solid tyred, outside staircase bodied trackless trolleybus was no. 17 (ON 3261), which was a prototype AEC 607 with a Vickers H26/26RO body, entering service during March 1926. It was withdrawn in August 1932, having covered some 99,585 miles, though for the last year it had only run about 3900 miles. It had the distinction of being the first trolleybus in the fleet to have a foot controller i.e. an accelerator. In 1926, the bodywork was totally up-to-date, but quickly looked dated. (AEC)

111. The Guy bodied Guy BTX, which was demonstrated to Birmingham for just one week between 10th and 17th April 1931 was 19 (OG 9886). The trolleybus was different from its Birmingham twin, UK 8341, as it had a straight staircase. It later became Llanelly & District's no. 16 in December 1934 being referred to in the local press as "the latest type of trolleybus operating on the Nechells route, Birmingham".
(Birmingham Evening Despatch)

112. At the outer turning circle at the Brampton terminus in Chesterfield in 1931 is the very first Leyland double decker to be built. A speculative venture, the vehicle was funded by Leyland Motors, GEC Witton and Birmingham Tramways and Omnibus Department. The chassis was designated as a TB1 and was registered OV 1175 with the fleet number 19. It was later converted to a Leyland "Titan" TD1 motorbus becoming Jersey Motor Traction's no. 24, registered J1199. It has the dubious distinction of being the only Birmingham trolleybus to be preserved, albeit as a motorbus! (A.J.Douglas)

113. Another trolleybus which was converted to a motorbus was OV 1194. This Guy BT with a Guy lowbridge 48 seater body ran in Birmingham from 20th to 31st March 1931 and in 1934, having languished in Fallings Park for three years, was converted to an FC petrol engined chassis. The "new" bus was then sold to Truman of Shirebrook, who ran it until 1947 when a new Guy "Arab" II chassis replaced the converted trolleybus unit and the re-chassied bus was registered KRA 668. The strangely proportioned front upper saloon windows and the spacing of the saloon windows suggest what it might have looked like in its full front trolleybus form. (R.Marshall)

114. Fifty Metro-Cammell bodied Leyland TTD2 trolleybuses were ordered by Birmingham in 1933 for the conversion of the Coventry Road tram routes to trolleybus operation. Numbered 17-66, this contract was at the time the largest single batch of trolleybuses ever made in Britain, as well as being the biggest order for metal framed trolleybus bodies. On 13th November 1933, the trolleybuses were well on their way to being completed at the Metro-Cammell works in Saltley. (Birmingham Post)

115. Passing the Sir Tatton Sykes public house in Victoria Square, Wolverhampton is that Corporation's 222. Registered OC 6567 in Birmingham, this 59 seater Metro-Cammell bodied Sunbeam MS2 had begun life as a demonstrator from 10th February to 31st March 1934 with Birmingham where it was numbered 67. This low height chassis type had a number of development problems, which caused Sunbeam to call in the Receiver in 1934.
(D.R.Harvey coll.)

THE END AND AFTER

116. The last trolleybus to run on the Birmingham system was Leyland TB7 no. 90 (FOK 90). Driven by Frederick L.Gilks, it left Coventry Road depot at 10-45 pm and travelled into the City terminus in Albert Street for an 11-02 pm departure. The trolleybus carried the General Manager W.H.Smith, members of the Transport Committee and senior officials of the Transport Department. Trolleybus 90 was then driven to the City Boundary terminus and returned to Coventry Road depot arriving at 12-05 am on 1st July 1951. A depot party had started at about 8-30 pm and these were some of the staff who posed in front of the trolleybus. By 12-30 am the power was switched off for the last time. (Birmingham Post)

117. About 30 of the Birmingham trolleybus fleet stand in Bird's scrapyard in Stratford a few days after the trolleybuses had run their last journeys along Coventry Road in Birmingham. It looks as though Mr Bird has only to erect some overhead and he could run a service around Stratford with these trolleybuses. Devoid of destination blinds, fleet numbers, legal lettering and municipal crests, the trolleybuses look in remarkably good condition for vehicles about to be broken up. (Stratford Guild Library)

118. By December 1951 the Birmingham trolleybuses were still largely intact and eleven of them are lined up in Bird's yard. They look a little more weather beaten, but generally seen in reasonable condition. In would be another six months before any effort was made to break up these trolleybuses as negotiations to sell the four wheelers came to nothing. (D.F.Parker)

119. Not all of the 74 Coventry Road trolleybuses were collected from the depot on 30th June 1951. Eight six-wheelers, one of the COX-registered trolleybuses and three of the FOK batch went to Cunliffe of Handsworth for storage until there was space at Bird's Stratford yard. The solitary COX vehicle was no. 73 which had been the last official 94 service trolleybus and stands forlornly in Cunliffe's Wellington Road yard; it was not collected by Bird for nearly a year and was still just recognisable in the Stratford scrapyard as late as 1969. (D.R.Harvey coll.)

120. Birds of Stratford had attempted to sell the FOK registered trolleybuses to South Africa, but the deal fell through and only the bodies of nos. 83 and 90 were used again. Both were mounted on Bristol K6G chassis by Silcox of Pembroke Dock and the body of no. 90 was registered ODE 401. The front dash was cut to allow the fitting of the Bristol radiator leaving the rest of the body still recognisably one from a Birmingham trolleybus. ODE 401 stands in South Parade, Tenby alongside the castle. (D.R.Harvey coll.)

MP Middleton Press

Easebourne Lane, Midhurst, West Sussex.
GU29 9AZ   Tel:01730 813169

EVOLVING THE ULTIMATE RAIL ENCYCLOPEDIA

www.middletonpress.co.uk   email:info@middletonpress.co.uk
A-978 0 906520   B-978 1 873793   C-978 1 901706   D-978 1 904474   E-978 1 906008

OOP Out of print at time of printing - Please check availability   BROCHURE AVAILABLE SHOWING NEW TITLES

A
Abergavenny to Merthyr C 91 8
Abertillery and Ebbw Vale Lines D 84 5
Aldgate & Stepney Tramways B 70 1
Allhallows - Branch Line to A 62 8
Alton - Branch Lines to A 11 6
Andover to Southampton A 82 6
Ascot - Branch Lines around A 64 2
Ashburton - Branch Line to B 95 4
Ashford - Steam to Eurostar B 67 1
Ashford to Dover A 48 2
Austrian Narrow Gauge D 04 3
Avonmouth - BL around D 42 5
Aylesbury to Rugby D 91 3

B
Baker Street to Uxbridge D 90 6
Banbury to Birmingham D 27 2
Barking to Southend C 80 2
Barnet & Finchley Tramways B 93 0
Barry - Branch Lines around D 50 0
Basingstoke to Salisbury A 89 5
Bath Green Park to Bristol C 36 9
Bath to Evercreech Junction A 60 4
Bath Tramways B 86 2
Battle over Portsmouth 1940 A 29 1
Battle over Sussex 1940 A 79 6
Bedford to Wellingborough D 31 9
Betwixt Petersfield & Midhurst A 94 9
Bletchley to Cambridge D 94 4
Bletchley to Rugby E 07 9
Blitz over Sussex 1941-42 B 35 0
Bodmin - Branch Lines around B 83 1
Bognor at War 1939-45 B 59 6
Bombers over Sussex 1943-45 B 51 0
Bournemouth & Poole Trys B 47 3
Bournemouth to Evercreech Jn A 46 8
Bournemouth to Weymouth A 57 4 OOP
Bournemouth Trolleybuses C 10 9
Bradford Trolleybuses D 19 7
Brecon to Neath D 43 2
Brecon to Newport D 16 6
Brecon to Newtown E 06 2
Brickmaking in Sussex B 19 6 OOP
Brightons Tramways B 02 2 OOP
Brighton to Eastbourne A 16 1
Brighton to Worthing A 03 1
Brighton Trolleybuses D 34 0
Bristols Tramways B 57 2
Bristol to Taunton D 03 6
Bromley South to Rochester B 23 7
Bromsgrove to Birmingham D 87 6
Bromsgrove to Gloucester D 73 9
Brunel - A railtour of his achievements D 74 6
Bude - Branch Line to B 29 9
Burnham to Evercreech Jn A 68 0
Burton & Ashby Tramways C 51 2

C
Camberwell & West Norwood Tys B 22 0
Cambridge to Ely D 55 5
Canterbury - Branch Lines around B 58 9
Cardiff Trolleybuses D 64 7
Caterham & Tattenham Corner B 25 1
Changing Midhurst C 15 4
Chard and Yeovil - BLs around C 30 7
Charing Cross to Dartford A 75 8
Charing Cross to Orpington A 96 3
Cheddar - Branch Line to B 90 9
Cheltenham to Andover C 43 7
Cheltenham to Redditch D 81 4
Chesterfield Tramways D 37 1
Chesterfield Trolleybuses D 51 7
Chester Tramways E 04 8
Chichester to Peterborough D 07 4
Clapham & Streatham Trys B 97 8
Clapham Junction - 50 yrs C 06 2 OOP
Clapham Junction to Beckenham Jn B 36 7
Cleobury Mortimer - Branch Lines around E 18 5
Clevedon & Portishead - BLs to D 18 0
Collectors Trains, Trolleys & Trams D 29 6
Colonel Stephens D62 3
Cornwall Narrow Gauge D 56 2
Cowdray & Easebourne D 96 8
Crawley to Littlehampton A 34 5
Cromer - Branch Lines around C 26 6
Croydons Tramways B 42 8
Croydons Trolleybuses B 73 2 OOP
Croydon to East Grinstead B 48 0
Crystal Palace (HL) & Catford Loop A 87 1
Cyprus Narrow Gauge E13 0

D
Darlington to Newcastle D 98 2
Darlington Trolleybuses D 33 3
Dartford to Sittingbourne B 34 3
Derby Tramways D 17 3
Derby Trolleybuses C 72 7
Derwent Valley - Branch Line to the D 06 7
Devon Narrow Gauge E 09 3
Didcot to Banbury D 02 9
Didcot to Swindon C 84 0
Didcot to Winchester C 13 0
Dorset & Somerset Narrow Gauge D 76 0
Douglas to Peel C 88 8
Douglas to Port Erin C 55 0
Douglas to Ramsey D 39 5
Dovers Tramways B 24 4
Dover to Ramsgate A 78 9

E
Ealing to Slough C 42 0
Eastbourne to Hastings A 27 7 OOP
East Cornwall Mineral Railways D 22 7
East Croydon to Three Bridges A 53 6
East Grinstead - Branch Lines to A 07 9
East Ham & West Ham Tramways B 52 7
East Kent Light Railway A 61 1 OOP
East London - Branch Lines of C 44 4
East London Line B 80 0
East Ridings Secret Resistance D 21 0
Edgware & Willesden Tramways C 18 5
Effingham Junction - BLs around A 74 1
Eltham & Woolwich Tramways B 74 9 OOP
Ely to Kings Lynn C 53 6
Ely to Norwich C 90 1
Embankment & Waterloo Tramways B 41 1
Enfield & Wood Green Trys C 03 1 OOP
Enfield Town & Palace Gates - BL to D 32 6
Epsom to Horsham A 30 7
Euston to Harrow & Wealdstone C 89 5
Exeter & Taunton Tramways B 32 9
Exeter to Barnstaple B 15 2
Exeter to Newton Abbot C 49 9
Exeter to Tavistock B 69 5
Exmouth - Branch Lines to B 00 8

F
Fairford - Branch Line to A 52 9
Falmouth, Helston & St. Ives - BL to C 74 1
Fareham to Salisbury A 67 3
Faversham to Dover B 05 3
Felixstowe & Aldeburgh - BL to D 20 3
Fenchurch Street to Barking C 20 8
Festiniog - 50 yrs of enterprise C 83 3
Festiniog 1946-55 E 01 7 - PUB 21 APRIL
Festiniog in the Fifties B 68 8
Festiniog in the Sixties B 91 6
Finsbury Park to Alexandra Palace C 02 4
Frome to Bristol B 77 0
Fulwell - Trams, Trolleys & Buses D 11 1

G
Gloucester to Bristol D 35 7
Gloucester to Cardiff D 66 1
Gosport & Horndean Trys B 92 3
Gosport - Branch Lines around A 36 9
Great Yarmouth Tramways D 13 5
Greece Narrow Gauge D 72 2
Greenwich & Dartford Tramways B 14 5 OOP
Grimsby & Cleethorpes Trolleybuses D 86 9
Guildford to Redhill A 63 5 OOP

H
Hammersmith & Hounslow Trys C 33 8
Hampshire Narrow Gauge D 36 4
Hampshire Waterways A 84 0 OOP
Hampstead & Highgate Tramways B 53 4
Harrow to Watford D 14 2
Hastings to Ashford A 37 6
Hastings Tramways B 18 3
Hastings Trolleybuses B 81 7 OOP
Hawkhurst - Branch Line A 66 6
Hay-on-Wye - Branch Lines around D 92 0
Hayling - Branch Line to A 12 3
Haywards Heath to Seaford A 28 4
Hemel Hempstead - Branch Lines to D 88 3
Henley, Windsor & Marlow - BL to C77 2
Hereford to Newport D 54 8
Hexham to Carlisle D 75 3
Hitchin to Peterborough D 07 4
Holborn & Finsbury Tramways B 79 4
Holborn Viaduct to Lewisham A 81 9
Horsham - Branch Lines to A 02 4
Huddersfield Tramways B 95 1
Huddersfield Trolleybuses C 92 5
Hull Tramways D60 9
Hull Trolleybuses D 24 1
Huntingdon - Branch Lines around A 93 2

I
Ilford & Barking Tramways B 61 9
Ilford to Shenfield C 97 0
Ilfracombe - Branch Line to B 21 3
Ilkeston & Glossop Tramways D 40 1
Industrial Rlys of the South East A 09 3
Ipswich to Saxmundham C 41 3
Ipswich Trolleybuses D 59 3
Isle of Wight Lines - 50 yrs C 12 3

K
Keighley Tramways & Trolleybuses D 83 8
Kent & East Sussex Waterways A 72 X
Kent Narrow Gauge C 45 1
Kent Seaways - Hoys to Hovercraft D 79 1
Kidderminster to Shrewsbury E10 9
Kingsbridge - Branch Line to C 98 7
Kingston & Hounslow Loops A 83 3 OOP
Kingston & Wimbledon Tramways B 56 5
Kingswear - Branch Line to C 17 8

L
Lambourn - Branch Line to C 70 3
Launceston & Princetown - BL to C 19 2
Lewisham & Catford Tramways B 26 8 OOP
Lewisham to Dartford A 92 5
Lines around Wimbledon B 75 6
Liverpool Street to Chingford D 01 2
Liverpool Street to Ilford C 34 5
Liverpool Tramways - Eastern C 04 8
Liverpool Tramways - Northern C 46 8
Liverpool Tramways - Southern C 23 9
Llandudno & Colwyn Bay Tramways E 17 8
London Bridge to Addiscombe B 20 6
London Bridge to East Croydon A 58 1
London Chatham & Dover Railway A 88 8
London Termini - Past and Proposed D 00 5
London to Portsmouth Waterways B 43 5
Longmoor - Branch Lines to A 41 3
Looe - Branch Line to C 22 2
Ludlow to Hereford E 14 7
Lyme Regis - Branch Line to A 45 1
Lynton - Branch Line to B 04 6

M
Maidstone & Chatham Tramways B 40 4
Maidstone Trolleybuses C 00 0 OOP
March - Branch Lines around B 09 1
Margate & Ramsgate Tramways C 52 9
Marylebone to Rickmansworth D 58 3
Melton Constable to Yarmouth Beach E 03 1
Midhurst - Branch Lines around A 49 9
Midhurst - Branch Lines to A 01 7 OOP
Military Defence of West Sussex A 23 9
Military Signals, South Coast C 54 3
Minehead - Branch Line to A 80 2
Mitcham Junction Lines B 01 5
Mitchell & company C 59 8
Monmouthshire Eastern Valleys D 71 5
Moreton-in-Marsh to Worcester D 26 5
Moretonhampstead - BL to C 27 7
Mountain Ash to Neath D 80 7

N
Newbury to Westbury C 66 6
Newcastle to Hexham D 69 2
Newcastle Trolleybuses D 78 4
Newport (IOW) - Branch Lines to A 26 0
Newquay - Branch Lines to C 71 0
Newton Abbot to Plymouth C 60 4
Northern France Narrow Gauge C 75 8
North East German Narrow Gauge D 44 9
North Kent Tramways B 44 2
North London Line B 94 7
North Woolwich - BLs around C 65 9
Norwich Tramways C 40 6
Nottinghamshire & Derbyshire T/B D 63 0
Nottinghamshire & Derbyshire T/W D 53 1

O
Ongar - Branch Lines to E 05 5
Orpington to Tonbridge B 03 9 OOP
Oxford to Bletchley D57 9
Oxford to Moreton-in-Marsh D 15 9

P
Paddington to Ealing C 37 6
Paddington to Princes Risborough C 81 9
Padstow - Branch Line to B 54 1
Plymouth - BLs around B 98 5
Plymouth to St. Austell C 63 5
Pontypool to Mountain Ash D 65 4
Porthmadog 1954-94 - BL around B 31 2
Porthmadog to Blaenau B 50 3 OOP
Portmadoc 1923-46 - BL around B 13 8
Portsmouths Tramways B 72 5
Portsmouth to Southampton A 31 4
Portsmouth Trolleybuses C 73 4
Potters Bar to Cambridge D 70 8
Princes Risborough - Branch Lines to D 05 0
Princes Risborough to Banbury C 85 7

R
Railways to Victory C 16 1 OOP
Reading to Basingstoke B 27 5
Reading to Didcot C 79 6
Reading to Guildford A 47 5 OOP
Reading Tramways B 87 9
Reading Trolleybuses C 05 5
Redhill to Ashford A 73 4
Return to Blaenau 1970-82 C 64 2
Rickmansworth to Aylesbury D 61 6
Roman Roads of Hampshire D 67 8
Roman Roads of Kent E 02 4
Roman Roads of Surrey C 61 1
Roman Roads of Sussex C 48 2
Romneyrail C 32 1
Ryde to Ventnor A 19 2

S
Salisbury to Westbury B 39 8
Salisbury to Yeovil B 06 0 OOP
Saxmundham to Yarmouth C 69 7
Saxony Narrow Gauge D 47 0
Scarborough Tramways E 15 4
Seaton & Eastbourne Tramways B 76 3 OOP
Seaton & Sidmouth - Branch Lines to A 95 6
Secret Sussex Resistance B 82 4
SECR Centenary album C 11 6 OOP
Selsey - Branch Line to A 04 8
Sheerness - Branch Lines around B 16 9 OOP
Shepherds Bush to Uxbridge T/Ws C 28 4
Shrewsbury - Branch Line to A 86 4
Sierra Leone Narrow Gauge D 28 9
Sirhowy Valley Line E 12 3
Sittingbourne to Ramsgate A 90 1
Slough to Newbury C 56 7
Solent - Creeks, Crafts & Cargoes D 52 4
Southamptons Tramways B 33 6
Southampton to Bournemouth A 42 0
Southend-on-Sea Tramways B 28 2
Southern France Narrow Gauge C 47 5
Southwark & Deptford Tramways B 38 1
Southwold - Branch Line to A 15 4
South Eastern & Chatham Railways C 08 6
South London Line B 46 6
South London Tramways 1903-33 D 10 4
South London Tramways 1933-52 D 89 0
South Shields Trolleybuses E 11 6
St. Albans to Bedford D 08 1
St. Austell to Penzance C 67 3
St. Pancras to Barking D 68 5
St. Pancras to St. Albans C 78 9
Stamford Hill Tramways B 88 5
Steaming through Cornwall B 30 5 OOP
Steaming through Kent A 13 0 OOP
Steaming through the Isle of Wight A 56 7
Steaming through West Hants A 69 7
Stratford upon avon to Birmingham D 77 7
Stratford upon Avon to Cheltenham C 25 3
Strood to Paddock Wood B 12 1 OOP
Surrey Home Guard C 57 4
Surrey Narrow Gauge C 87 1
Surrey Waterways A 51 2 OOP
Sussex Home Guard C 24 6
Sussex Narrow Gauge C 68 0
Sussex Shipping Sail, Steam & Motor D 23 4 OOC
Swanley to Ashford B 45 9
Swindon to Bristol C 96 3
Swindon to Gloucester D46 3
Swindon to Newport D 30 2
Swiss Narrow Gauge C 94 9

T
Talyllyn - 50 years C 39 0
Taunton to Barnstaple B 08 2
Taunton to Exeter C 82 6
Tavistock to Plymouth B 88 6
Tees-side Trolleybuses D 58 6
Tenterden - Branch Line to A 21 5
Thanets Tramways B 11 4 OOP
Three Bridges to Brighton A 35 2
Tilbury Loop C 86 4
Tiverton - Branch Lines around C 62 8
Tivetshall to Beccles D 41 8
Tonbridge to Hastings A 44 4
Torrington - Branch Lines to B 37 4
Tunbridge Wells - Branch Lines to A 32 1
Twickenham & Kingston Trys C 35 2
Two-Foot Gauge Survivors C 21 5 OOP

U
Upwell - Branch Line to B 64 0

V
Victoria & Lambeth Tramways B 49 7
Victoria to Bromley South A 98 7
Victoria to East Croydon A 40 6 OOP
Vivarais C 31 4 OOP
Vivarais Revisited E 08 6

W
Walthamstow & Leyton Tramways B 65 7
Waltham Cross & Edmonton Trys C 07 9
Wandsworth & Battersea Tramways B 63 3
Wantage - Branch Line to D 25 8
Wareham to Swanage - 50 yrs D 09 8
War on the Line A 10 9
War on the Line VIDEO + 88 0
Waterloo to Windsor A 54 3
Waterloo to Woking A 38 3
Watford to Leighton Buzzard D 45 6
Wenford Bridge to Fowey C 09 3
Westbury to Bath B 55 8
Westbury to Taunton C 76 5
West Cornwall Mineral Railways D 48 7
West Croydon to Epsom B 08 4
West German Narrow Gauge D 93 7
West London - Branch Lines of C 50 5
West London Line B 84 8
West Sussex Waterways A 24 6 OOP
West Wiltshire - Branch Lines of D 12 8
Weymouth - Branch Lines around A 65 9
Willesden Junction to Richmond B 71 8
Wimbledon to Beckenham C 58 1
Wimbledon to Epsom B 62 6
Wimborne - Branch Lines around A 97 0
Wisbech - Branch Lines around C 01 7
Wisbech 1800-1901 C 93 2
Woking to Alton A 59 8
Woking to Portsmouth A 25 3
Woking to Southampton A 55 0
Wolverhampton Trolleybuses D 85 2
Woolwich & Dartford Trolleys B 66 4
Worcester to Birmingham D 97 5
Worcester to Hereford D 38 8
Worthing to Chichester A 06 2

Y
Yeovil - 50 yrs change C 38 3
Yeovil to Dorchester A 76 5 OOP
Yeovil to Exeter A 91 8
York Tramways & Trolleybuses D 82 1